MOOCS

JONATHAN HABER

The MIT Press | Cambridge, Massachusetts | London, England

MIT Press books may be purchased at special quantity discounts for business or sales promotional use. For information, please email special_sales@mitpress.mit.edu

This book was set in Chaparral by the MIT Press. Printed and bound in the United States of America.

Library of Congress Cataloging-in-Publication Data

Haber, Jonathan.
MOOCs / Jonathan Haber.
    pages   cm—(The MIT Press essential knowledge series)
Includes bibliographical references and index.
ISBN 978-0-262-52691-3 (pbk. : alk. paper)
1. MOOCs (Web-based instruction) 2. Distance education. 3. Web-based instruction. 4. Computer-assisted instruction. 5. Educational technology.
I. Title.
LB1044.87.H27 2014
371.33'44678—dc23

                                                        2014013238

10 9 8 7 6 5 4 3 2 1

CONTENTS

SERIES FOREWORD

The MIT Press Essential Knowledge series offers accessible, concise, beautifully produced pocket-size books on topics of current interest. Written by leading thinkers, the books in this series deliver expert overviews of subjects that range from the cultural and the historical to the scientific and the technical.

In today's era of instant information gratification, we have ready access to opinions, rationalizations, and superficial descriptions. Much harder to come by is the foundational knowledge that informs a principled understanding of the world. Essential Knowledge books fill that need. Synthesizing specialized subject matter for nonspecialists and engaging critical topics through fundamentals, each of these compact volumes offers readers a point of access to complex ideas.

Bruce Tidor
Professor of Biological Engineering and Computer Science
Massachusetts Institute of Technology

I walked into the evening cocktail hour (still charmingly referred to as a "smoker") at the 2013 American Philosophical Association (APA) Eastern Division Conference even more self-conscious than the job-hunting graduate students nervously prowling the halls. For they at least had PhDs, while my philosophical training consisted of just one year of intense study—study conducted entirely online, facilitated by massive open online courses (MOOCs) and other forms of free learning.

That field trip served as the final exam for a program that began a year earlier when I had just finished an online class in logic and argumentation entitled Think Again: How to Reason and Argue, offered by Duke University through a company called Coursera. And, after completing the course, it was clear to me that something new and potentially revolutionary was happening in education.

Despite being free, the online class was as good (i.e., as thorough and rigorous) as a college course on the same subject I recall taking as an undergraduate in the 1980s. And apparently this combination of "free" and "good" led over 100,000 other people to enroll in the class alongside me.

As it turns out, I was participating in a MOOC, one of the fastest growing and most talked-about trends in higher education.

Unlike previous stories of educational transformation that played out haltingly over years or even decades, the rise of the MOOC was occurring within the highly compressed timeframe of an Internet phenomenon. MOOCs were all but unknown outside of the work of a few education specialists in the summer of 2011 when Stanford University decided to open up Web-based versions of some of its most popular computer science courses to the world. And when enrollment in those classes climbed into the hundreds of thousands, a major education and technology news story—not to mention a new market opportunity—was born.

That market opportunity was seized upon by the very Stanford professors whose courses first drew those outstanding numbers, including Sebastian Thrun, who founded Udacity, and Andrew Ng, who founded Coursera along with his Stanford colleague Daphne Koller. And not to be outdone by these West Coast startups, Harvard and MIT each invested millions to create the nonprofit MOOC provider edX in May 2012.

So by the time I had enrolled in Coursera's Think Again, there were already hundreds of massive online courses being taken by millions of students around the globe. And the combination of huge student enrollments, millions of investment dollars, and decisions by name-brand universities to start giving courses away for free made MOOCs a red-hot educational news topic for both the education and mainstream media.

Early coverage seemed positively giddy at the thought of MOOCs disrupting a traditional college experience often condemned for being both overpriced and trapped in the past. Star columnist Thomas Friedman dedicated multiple *New York Times* opinion pieces to the subject,[1] highlighting a comparison made by Harvard Business School professor Clayton Christensen (a specialist in the impact of disruptive technologies) between today's colleges and universities and General Motors in the 1960s—with MOOCs serving the role of Toyota. And MOOC providers were no less bold with their pronouncements, such as when Udacity's Sebastian Thrun was quoted in *Wired* magazine declaring that in fifty years there would be only ten institutions in the world delivering higher education.[2]

Unsurprisingly, this type of technological utopianism prompted a backlash, and by the spring of 2013 the naysayers were in the ascendant, declaring MOOCs to be both academically worthless and a threat to the entire edifice of higher education.

Having had a positive (albeit not yet life-transforming) experience with my first MOOC class, much of this debate seemed to be both extreme and uninformed. Most of the people engaged in these arguments and counterarguments, be they college administrators and educational policymakers or teachers and students, seemed united in not having much experience with real live MOOCs, except for professors who may have taught one or students who enrolled in—and may have even completed—one or two.

The voice I felt was missing in these heated yet vital discussions was that of a student who had not simply dabbled in MOOC courses, but who had completed enough of them to be able to determine how well the experience as a whole compared to a traditional college education.

It was then that those three words that tend to send shudders through my household were uttered: "Why not me?"

And so I began my own experiment within the greater MOOC experiment called Degree of Freedom,[3] which required me to complete the same number of courses one would take to obtain a four-year liberal arts degree in just twelve months using only MOOCs and other forms of free learning.

While that undergraduate degree I had earned in the 1980s (at Wesleyan University) was in chemistry, my interests have since moved more toward history and the humanities. That, combined with curiosity over whether MOOCs could cut it beyond the computer science subjects they are still most famous for led me to organize my one-year BA project around a liberal arts major (philosophy).

While an important goal of this experiment was to quickly acquire and communicate the types of student-centric experiences one can gain only by trying the widest possible range of platforms, institutions, subjects, and professors, work on Degree of Freedom also brought me into contact with the people deeply engaged with the

MOOC experiment, including the founders of the major MOOC providers, instructors pushing the edges of online learning, and students of all ages creating their own unconventional learning paths.

It was through this intense process of studying, writing, and discussion (which I eventually realized constituted a second major, in MOOCs, with this book serving as my "senior thesis") that I realized massive open online courses were neither a panacea to the "crisis in education" (a crisis people are far happier to rail against than define) nor the terrifying threat condemned by doomsayers. Rather, they represent a phenomenon following along a well-worn timeline for initially overhyped but still transformative technologies that eventually find a "plateau of productivity" from which they can do their slow-but-steadily disruptive work.

This book is designed to provide background and guidance to anyone interested in or trying to navigate his or her own way through the thicket of competing claims, aspirations, and accusations that still clutter discussion of an important new educational technology, a technology that stands a chance of transforming many (albeit not all) aspects of learning for the better, but only if the MOOC experiment continues long enough to deliver its potential benefits.

I would like to thank all of those participating in this experiment, including the professors, teaching teams, and fellow students from whom I learned so much. Thanks to the organizations and companies that have made an investment in free learning for all, including people working at the MOOC providers who helped with the research for this book. Thanks also to Marc Lowenthal, Marie Lee, Michael Sims and the rest of the MIT Press team for their help and encouragement. To Lee McIntyre: thanks for instilling in me a love for philosophy. Thanks to Hilary Mitchell who designed my Degree of Freedom web site and to Kristin Griffin who came up with a name for that project. And special thinks to my wife Carolyn and my entire family for their patience and support during this year-long journey.

INTRODUCTION

In the summer of 2011, professors at Stanford University decided to offer video versions of three computer science classes, originally delivered via the school's OpenClassroom learning portal, to the world. Excitement was high that this experiment might attract hundreds, maybe as many as a few thousand, students.

By the time the first of those courses began in the fall, enrollments had topped 160,000.

The professors behind this project recognized an opportunity when they saw one. And by spring semester of 2012, the "Year of the MOOC" had begun.

MOOC, which stands for massive open online course, became one of those rare phenomena: an education innovation that captures the imagination of the public at large while moving at the speed of an Internet startup.

Generally, technology has entered the educational ecosystem at a more deliberate pace. For instance, products such as learning management systems (also called "LMSs"),

MOOC, which stands for massive open online course, became one of those rare phenomena: an education innovation that captures the imagination of the public at large while moving at the speed of an Internet startup.

which automate the interaction between a school's students, teachers, and administrators, and Internet-driven distance-learning programs, have only gone mainstream after the usual deliberation among stakeholders and the piloting associated with most technology initiatives. And while these technologies have indeed transformed the learning landscape, only avid readers of education- or educational-technology-specific publications would have been aware of the ups and downs of their integration into the classroom.

Not so for MOOCs, which seem to have struck a chord not just with educators but with the public at large.

The just-mentioned "Year of the MOOC" title was given to 2012 by the *New York Times*[1] to highlight a year during which Sebastian Thrun (the man behind Stanford's artificial intelligence class—enrollment 160,000) founded KnowLabs (now Udacity) and promised to bring more free massive classes to the world.

Following right behind Thrun were Andrew Ng (who taught Stanford's equally popular machine learning course, also with an enrollment over 100,000) and his fellow Stanford Professor Daphne Koller (a MacArthur award–winning Artificial Intelligence research scientist), who together launched Coursera in April 2012 and immediately began forming partnerships with colleges and universities around the world that allowed them to leverage Coursera technology to give "rock star professors" the chance to educate thousands.

Some argued that MOOCs were an innovation that could have emerged only from the startup culture of Silicon Valley, but educators at prestigious East Coast universities weren't buying it. After all, the Massachusetts Institute of Technology had been offering access to nearly all of its teaching materials (including lecture videos and notes, syllabi, and even homework exercises and exam materials) via its OpenCourseWare initiative for a decade.[2] So rather than joining the queue behind other universities signing deals with venture-funded for-profit companies like Udacity or Coursera, MIT instead teamed up with Harvard to create their own competing MOOC provider: edX, a non-profit begun with commitments of more than fifty million dollars from the two Cambridge-based educational giants.

When large institutions that normally move into new educational arenas at a glacial pace start writing multimillion-dollar checks to try to quickly compete in an emerging market, that's a story of interest to more than just the educational media. And the fact that some of the nation's most prestigious colleges and universities spent 2012 and 2013 lining up to deliver classes via one of the emerging East- or West-Coast MOOC-consortia established MOOCs as something that could not be dismissed as a passing educational fad.

In fact, for all of the discussion of money and technology that have played out in both the educational and mainstream press since the MOOC story broke, the most significant aspect of the rise of MOOCs may turn out to be the changes they have wrought within the culture of higher education where institutions that once hoarded their classroom experiences as valuable intellectual assets were suddenly rushing to share that content with the world.

As my Degree of Freedom project was wrapping up toward the end of 2013, the "Big Three" MOOC providers—Udacity, Coursera, and edX—were offering over 500 courses on varying disciplines, with total enrollment in MOOC classes topping seven million. Meanwhile, new international competitors such as FutureLearn (an offshoot of Britain's venerable distance-learning provider Open University) and Germany's iversity were entering the MOOC provider market while other companies offering paid courses alongside free educational content were stretching the boundaries of what constituted a "genuine" MOOC.

But if 2012 was "The Year of the MOOC," even if MOOCs were far fewer and more primitive during their first year than they are today, 2013 turned out to be the year of the MOOC backlash.

Rumblings against this "new new thing" in education began in April of that year when Amherst College decided to take a "wait-and-see" attitude toward joining a MOOC partnership.[3] And while this decision didn't prevent other schools (including Yale, which signed up with Coursera a month later) from taking the plunge, the Amherst decision communicated that participating in the "MOOC movement" was not necessarily a requirement for every respectable institution of higher learning fretful of being left behind.

The benefits of free, open education for all were hard to dismiss when the first MOOC classes were emerging. But once those classes had been in the field for a few semesters, there was suddenly data both boosters and critics of MOOCs could use to support their pro- and anti-MOOC arguments.

For critics, high attrition rates were an easy target, given that fewer than 10 percent of people who signed up for a MOOC tended to take it to completion. And once institutions moved from agreeing to create a MOOC to actually building and delivering one, the amount of work involved, not to mention the challenges inherent in trying to teach tens of thousands of students simultaneously (all while balancing other teaching responsibilities), became the basis for a new set of concerns.

Tales of flame wars breaking out in the online comment forums, originally designed to replicate the civil discourse of the classroom, were part of that story, as were disappointments over the lack of engagement of many students, which caused one UC Irvine professor to abandon his course midsemester out of frustration.[4]

And then there was the natural conflict between the claimed altruistic missions of MOOC providers to educate the planet and the need for these organizations to make money out of what was emerging as a massive Internet giveaway. Usual methods of "monetizing eyeballs" (such as online ads) seemed anathema to the culture of education, but proposed business models that would allow venture-funded companies to turn a profit (or nonprofits that could not expect institutional backing to go on forever to sustain themselves) led to suspicions that MOOCs could end up decimating traditional education in order to generate a return for investors or, in the case of nonprofits, generate the funds needed to achieve self-sufficiency.

One business model that has been actively explored by MOOC providers, licensing content to residential institutions of higher education such as state and community colleges, created the biggest MOOC controversy of 2013 when professors in the philosophy department of San Jose State University published a letter, ostensibly written to Harvard professor Michael Sandel (one of the aforementioned "rock star professors" who teaches the popular ethics class Justice for edX), complaining that the school's licensing of edX content was part of a scheme by administrators to replace paid faculty with third-party video lectures.[5] In fact, suspicion over this still largely experimental licensing model led one instructor of a popular Coursera course to pull his support from the project when the chance came to give the class a second time.[6]

As MOOCs were going through this roller-coaster ride over the course of 2013, I was in the unusual position of standing still while public opinion was changing around me. For my cautious enthusiasm over what massive open learning might eventually evolve into was neither zealous enough for those celebrating a MOOC revolution, nor cynical enough to suit those participating in the backlash. More important, as someone with experience watching popular technology trends play out in fields outside the politically fraught world of education, this trajectory of zeal followed by paranoia was fitting into a familiar trend: that of the "Hype Cycle" for new, disruptive technologies.

This Hype Cycle model (figure 1), originally developed by the Gartner Group technology-consulting firm,[7] maps out important peaks and valleys of perception that tend to repeat whenever an important technology-driven trend plays out.

According to this model, a "technology trigger" of some sort introduces something new into an established marketplace. This trigger might be a new invention, but more frequently it is the result of a once-experimental or peripheral technology becoming affordable or stable enough to become accepted as a standard.

For instance, e-book technology had existed for years in the form of products from different vendors who had created their own standards and devices, companies that struggled to build relationships with established publishers while working out new business models for book sales and distribution. But it was Amazon's release of the

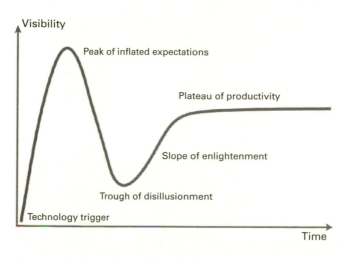

Figure 1   The Gartner Group's Hype Cycle

Kindle, a standard rapidly embraced by large numbers of major publishers, that served as the technology trigger for mainstreaming the replacement of older production and delivery systems (print, warehouse, delivery truck, and bookstore) with something new (the tablet reader fed by Internet download).

In the case of MOOCs, it was the emergence of companies like Udacity, Coursera, and edX, whose technologies could facilitate classes taken by tens of thousands, that triggered a MOOC movement that had previously been relegated to theoretical frameworks or experimental courses, some of which are described further in chapter 2.

Once such new and promising technologies grab public attention, the next stage involves inflated expectations that tend to minimize any potential downside in favor of visions of a near-term utopia.

For e-books, the notion of instant gratification coupled with lower-cost fed expectations that any publisher that remained attached to print in any way was doomed to oblivion, especially in a world where writers could bypass publishers entirely to self-publish directly to the Kindle or to competing technologies like Apple's iPad or Barnes and Noble's Nook.

MOOCs passed through this "Inflated Expectations" stage in 2012 when 100,000+ person enrollments in newly emerging massive classes fueled expectations that Harvard- or Stanford-quality education would soon be available to all for free, solving problems such as third-world poverty abroad and the skyrocketing cost of higher education at home—if not immediately, then at least over that fifty-year period Udacity founder Sebastian Thrun predicted would be needed before MOOCs came to rule an educational landscape consisting of no more than ten institutions.

Unsurprisingly, it was this very vision that terrified those professors who feared they might not be working in one of those ten theoretically surviving schools. But even absent an entrenched establishment threatened by disruptive technology, inflated expectations invariably lead to disappointment (or, in Hype Cycle terminology, a "Trough of Disillusionment") as euphoric fantasies run head-on into the realities associated with the introduction of any transformative innovation.

Continuing with the e-book parallel, this technology was greeted with an initial backlash by those passionate about traditional printed books (a substantial group with significant cultural influence). But disillusionment with e-book technology was not simply fueled by nostalgia. For e-books—with their eccentric form factors, layout limitations, and live (i.e., distracting) "hot links"—were proving to offer a different and not necessarily superior reading experience compared to the printed book. And as authors realized that their self-published Kindle editions were being downloaded by only a few family members, the role played by traditional publishers beyond layout, manufacturing, and delivery, especially with regard to building awareness of new titles, became apparent to authors and publishers alike.

In the case of MOOCs, the challenges inherent in delivering quality courses to huge numbers demonstrated that digital videos of Harvard lectures did not a Harvard education make. More pragmatically, MOOC courses seemed to vary enormously in terms of quality and workload. And with no clear way to ensure that a student enrolled in a MOOC was the one actually doing the work, it was difficult to claim that any massive open course constituted the equivalent of a traditional semester-long college class.

In cases where college equivalency was claimed (or even proven), the complex process of turning MOOCs into genuine college credit made it an option for just an industrious few. And even when MOOC providers established programs to smooth the way toward obtaining credit via an established institution, few if any students signed up, indicating that the audience for MOOCs might actually not be college students seeking an alternative to a traditional—and expensive—education.

As these genuine concerns met with some of the suspicion and paranoia mentioned earlier, a MOOC backlash occurred that sometimes manifested itself as outright hostility but was mostly expressed as cooling interest in MOOCs as a whole, which is why MOOC news stories toward the end of 2013 were far fewer than what we saw at the beginning of that year.

The point of the Gartner Hype Cycle curve is to demonstrate that neither the height of inflated expectations nor the trough of disillusionment are particularly productive with regard to allowing a new technology to find its proper fit in the marketplace. For that to happen, cooler heads need to prevail that are willing to embrace the new technology—warts and all—and allow it to evolve to the point where it can achieve its potential. For just as e-book technology now coexists with older methods of production and distribution while also evolving to create new and unique reading experiences, so too can massive open

Even when MOOC providers established programs to smooth the way toward obtaining credit via an established institution, few students signed up, indicating that the audience might not be college students seeking an alternative to a traditional—and expensive—education.

classes usher in an exciting (if not utopian) educational future, but only if the MOOC experiment is allowed to run its course.

Finding the proper pathway up this "Slope of Enlightenment" to allow MOOCs to more rapidly reach a "Plateau of Productivity" was the goal of my Degree of Freedom project, which provided ground-level, student-centric understanding of what worked and what didn't in real, live MOOC classes. It is also the goal of this book, which should be thought of as a means to shorten and steepen the enlightenment curve by providing perspective on how MOOCs came about, what they consist of, their issues, challenges, and potential futures.

This effort begins in chapter 2, which attempts to place MOOCs into a broader context of trends in traditional and online learning. On the surface, MOOCs might just seem like general online courses, albeit with no fees and huge open enrollments. But by seeing where MOOCs fit into the evolutionary history of online education, we can determine how closely the MOOCs taken today by millions of students fit (or don't fit) the vision of earlier pioneers in technology-driven teaching and learning.

Chapter 3 looks at the components of a MOOC (such as lectures, assessment, and homework) to see what techniques and technologies underlie the ability to package this material and deliver it to hundreds of thousands. This chapter also addresses some key questions regarding whether a course can simply be thought of as the sum of its constituent parts. And in an era when companies outside the original MOOC "big three" are repackaging and rebranding existing content as massive online course offerings, we take a look at the question of how to best define "MOOC" and consider what might determine whether an online course fits into this category.

Chapter 4 looks at some of the issues and controversies associated with MOOCs, including the high dropout rates and college credit equivalency questions that have made news. But the emergence of massive open learning also raises equally important, if less public, debates over matters such as intellectual property and open access. An understanding of matters beyond and behind the headlines is vital to anyone trying to understand or make decisions that take into account the plusses and minuses of massive open learning.

Much of the writing surrounding this subject uses the phrase "the MOOC experiment" to highlight the fact that individual MOOCs, as well as the MOOC concept as a whole, should be thought of as an experimental program playing out in public rather than a product being presented as already perfected. Although cynics could dismiss this language as a means to excuse releasing sloppy or unfinished work into the marketplace, the scientific attitude expressed by MOOCs being an experiment in new learning methods is deeply embedded in the DNA of those most heavily invested in their success. Chapter 5 takes a deeper look at the research and experimentation taking place within individual massive classes and what such a culture of experimentation might contribute to the overall MOOC project.

Finally, chapter 6 looks at trends that are playing out with regard to who is using MOOCs and for what purpose to map out potential futures for massive open learning if it does manage to reach a "Plateau of Productivity."

The "perfect is the enemy of the good" is a phrase attributed to Voltaire, although that sentiment can be seen in the work of other thinkers before and since. And in the highly charged, highly politicized, high-stakes world of education, innovation and reform are frequently criticized for providing "only" partial or gradual solutions to some of the many problems that plague education, such as lack of results, high cost, and limited access to resources, rather than providing immediate answers to all of them.

It is difficult to argue that no good can come out of the world's most successful colleges and universities making classes taught by skilled and enthusiastic professors eager to share their knowledge available to anyone with an Internet connection. But even if we can avoid the fallacy of thinking that because MOOCs cannot solve all our educational challenges they aren't worth pursuing, we still need to understand the nature of the benefits such programs deliver as well as who can benefit from them.

As with any book covering a fast-moving topic, there is always the risk that the words I'm writing now might seem outdated by the time you read them, especially since MOOCs (like many inventions that have come before) are a collection of technologies moving in directions even their creators never anticipated. But with a grounding in where MOOCs came from, what they consist of, what challenges they face, and where they might be going, readers will stand a better chance of making better decisions regarding their own involvement with this promising and still potentially revolutionary new method of learning.

WHERE DID MOOCS COME FROM?

When looking for precedents regarding the symbiosis between technology and education, one could go back to the Protestant Reformation in sixteenth-century Europe when a new communication technology, the printing press, became associated with a theology that stressed personal study of the bible, which the new printing technology made more widely available. This historic combination created the need for a more widely literate public, a need that could be met only by expanding education beyond clerics and aristocrats.

But it was the value later Enlightenment figures placed on universal education that led to the creation of public school systems as well as the massive expansion of institutions of higher learning from the eighteenth century onward. These Enlightenment-era thinkers also embraced science as a road to progress in all aspects of human life, a faith that only became more intense in the nineteenth and twentieth centuries when technology was revolutionizing existing industries, such as agriculture and transportation, while creating a host of new activities like automated factory production and global commodities trade. In addition to disrupting established methods of manufacturing and commerce, these innovations also created the need for increasing numbers of educated managers and technocrats.

Faith in the combined virtues of universal education and technical progress meant that from the nineteenth century onward, any new breakthrough in communications technology was almost immediately put to work toward the goal of educating the masses, with MOOCs being just the latest manifestation of this historic impulse.

Distance Education

When MOOCs are discussed in the context of distance education, an analogy is often drawn to correspondence courses first popularized in the 1840s by the UK's Sir Isaac Pittman, whose correspondence colleges offered to train students in his new shorthand method by sending them instruction manuals through the mail.[1]

This early iteration of education by post created an industry that continues to this day. Those of us who grew up in the 1960s and 1970s may associate correspondence classes with invitations to draw Winky the Deer or Lucky the Duck appearing on matchbooks or in ads in popular magazines, the recruitment method for Art Instruction Inc., a correspondence school founded in 1914 that offers art instruction by mail.[2] But correspondence classes were also the means by which major universities tried to fulfill their mission for educational outreach.

In the late 1800s, for example, US schools such as Illinois Wesleyan, the University of Chicago (under the leadership of distance education pioneer William Rainley Harper[3]), and the University of Wisconsin all offered degree programs through the mail. The concentration of such programs in the Midwest reflected a mission for many of these newly created institutions to support educational outreach to rural communities that lacked easy access to the resources of a major urban campus. These distance education programs were also heavily involved with government programs at the federal and state level (such as the creation of the Extension Service and foundation of Land Grant Colleges), which tried to improve the conditions of Americans living in underserved agricultural regions. The undergraduate and even graduate degree-by-mail opportunities these schools offered also opened up opportunities for educational advancement to other dispersed communities such as military personnel.

The technological breakthroughs that made correspondence-based education possible during this era were

Faith in the combined
virtues of universal
education and technical
progress meant that
from the nineteenth
century onward,
any new breakthrough
in communications

technology was almost immediately put to work toward the goal of educating the masses, with MOOCs being just the latest manifestation of this historic impulse.

infrastructural (such as the expansion of rail and road networks, which enabled the mail to reach every home) and mechanical (the machine-powered printing press, which dramatically lowered the cost of printed books).

Low-cost printing, which was made possible as a result of modern farming and manufacturing techniques in the paper industry, fueled other informal means of bringing educational content to previously marginalized communities. Public libraries, for example, which expanded into every community in the nineteenth and twentieth centuries, were able to stock inexpensively produced books that a growing publishing industry was churning out in ever greater numbers. This technology-driven downward price spiral also meant books were finding their way into private hands through familiar commercial channels such as bookstores and modern distribution techniques such as the traveling salesman.[4]

Low-cost print and distribution opened up other avenues for books to reach the masses. To cite one example, my father (a retired professor of literature) discovered what we would now term "The Great Books" in the library of *his* father, a factory foreman who had obtained them free as part of his subscription to *PM*, a left-leaning New York news daily that decided access to the classics was essential to uplifting members of the working class.

Electronic Media

Broadcast media, first radio in the 1920s and then television in the 1950s, created opportunities for important partnerships between newly emerging broadcasters hungry for content, skilled lecturers with an interest in reaching a wider audience, and national governments interested in ensuring a public education mission for the broadcast spectrum they were licensing and regulating.

In the United States, this mission took the form of licensing radio stations at educational institutions (over 200 such licenses were granted between 1918 and 1946). But formal education via this medium failed to catch on (by 1940, the only college course offered by radio had no takers).[5] Television fared somewhat better in the educational arena with programs such as *Sunrise Semester* (which ran on the CBS broadcast network from 1957 through 1982), allowing New York University to offer for-credit courses on a range of disciplines to students willing to sit through enough 6 am lectures.

As advances in recording technology lowered costs of production and distribution of audio (via inexpensive LPs, cassette tapes, and eventually audio CDs), and video (via Beta, then VHS video tape, and finally DVDs), these media became yet another means to distribute educational content. And distance education organizations were quick to embrace these new technologies, as were businesses eager to find new worker-training methods that were less expensive and disruptive than live classes run during work hours.

Recorded college lectures continue to be popular, as reflected by the success of products such as the Great Courses series by The Teaching Company or the Modern Scholar lectures by Recorded Books, both offering lecture courses in a variety of college-level disciplines via CD, DVD, and Internet download. And Apple's iTunes U service, which allows people to download audio and video recordings of live college classes, has been a popular part of the company's media offerings since 2007.

But lectures alone, either broadcast or recorded (or in the classroom, for that matter), were never enough to constitute the entirety of an educational experience, which is why it required a new generation of distance-learning pioneers to come up with new pedagogies that would stitch together the various components of a class, including lectures, reading assignments, graded homework, and tests, into something recognizable as a complete and genuine "course."

While the first steps in this direction were taken by schools such as the University of South Africa (which began offering degrees at a distance in 1962), the most well-known example of a virtual campus that leveraged each new communication technology as it became available is the UK's Open University (OU), which took in its first students in 1971.[6]

In addition to embracing radio, television, audio and video recordings, and eventually the Internet as educational communication tools, Open University, unlike similar distance education initiatives at the time, had no formal entrance requirements beyond the ability to pay (often subsidized) and willingness to participate in classes and complete assignments. And while the digital computing and Internet technologies that would eventually underlie MOOCs were not in existence as Open University grew to serve hundreds of thousands of students in its first decades, OU's program represents one of the first instances of the no-barriers philosophy that would become a cornerstone of massive online learning.

Computer-Based Teaching

Early attempts to integrate technology into the classroom—one of the most interesting being B. F. Skinner's Teaching Machine,[7] a mechanical device that would feed content to students using a predetermined algorithm—never got much traction in the primary grades it was envisioned to serve. But such inventions did create a template for subsequent devices and techniques to come that would use technology to diverge from the one-size-fits-all-at-the-same-time pedagogies that formed the basis of traditional classroom education.

It took the introduction of the digital computer, which offered information storage and sharing resources that facilitated communications and interaction, to provide a platform that would eventually replace disparate educational modalities (such as lectures on audio or video tape, readings delivered by mail, or exams taken on site) with a single point of entry for most if not all of the distance education experience.

Like all of the technologies mentioned so far in this chapter, the computer was embraced almost immediately as an educational instrument—this despite severe limitations of early devices, which consisted of large centralized systems with which students interacted primarily via terminals capable of displaying only text-based characters.

PLATO (standing for Programmed Logic for Automatic Teaching Operations), a system developed in the 1960s by professors at the University of Illinois, is probably the most important early attempt to apply new computing technologies to challenges in education.[8] While built on networked mainframe systems that primarily time-sliced character-based content to "dumb" terminals, PLATO evolved to incorporate elements its creators decided were crucial to education. For example, the need to display graphics as well as text led PLATO's builders to innovate precursors to the graphical user interface eventually taken up by computer scientists at Xerox PARC, innovations that ultimately found their way into the Apple Macintosh and Windows systems we today take for granted. And the importance of facilitating professor-to-student and student-to-student communication led PLATO's makers to construct technologies that prefigured and inspired electronic mail, bulletin board systems, and all of the other online communications facilities that underlie today's hyperconnected world.

As computers went through their rapid evolution from centralized systems based on mainframe and minicomputers connected to "dumb" terminals through low-cost and autonomous microcomputers to today's powerful networked machines, education continued to find new uses for each advance in computing technology.

For example, early microcomputers that ran character-based operating systems (such as the Apple II and IBM PC running DOS) or graphical operating systems (like the Macintosh or IBM PCs and clones running Microsoft Windows) were embraced by home and school users as educational tools that could run standalone teaching software, including educational games, flashcards, and automated homework exercises. But it was the networked communication facilitated by the Internet's rise in the 1990s that turned computing technology from a support tool to a potential replacement for the traditional classroom.

It should be noted that by the time the Internet (first created in the 1960s) started to enter the mainstream, previous limitations associated with desktop computers were becoming a thing of the past. For instance, plummeting hardware costs meant computers with enough memory and storage capacity to run multimedia applications like audio and video had become commodities. And by the time a new generation of online universities opened its doors, high-speed bandwidth was also becoming available and affordable (at least in the developed world) as the once familiar modem whistle followed by a blast of static was replaced by instantly available audio and video content from, among other places, institutions of learning.

Education has been transformed not only through advances in technology but by advances in teaching methodology and pedagogy, by educational reform movements (many emphasizing outcomes and testing), and by political decisions regarding how to prioritize the substantial sums government invests in education at the local, state/regional, and national levels. And even as these new ways of teaching and learning have been influenced by a rapidly expanding educational technology industry, they have also provided the intellectual foundation upon which many EdTech ventures have been built.

Any one of these topics deserves its own historical account. But for purposes of continuing this chapter's storyline leading to the emergence of the MOOC, a list of relevant innovations related to online learning that started in the 1990s includes the following:

• The introduction of learning management systems (LMSs) into college campuses, which automated the interaction between students and professors (through features such as automated distribution of syllabus material and submission of homework assignments), as well as professors and administrators (through systems such as centralized grading and reporting).

• The creation of a new generation of distance-teaching providers that today use the Internet as their primary content-delivery mechanism, one of the most well known being the University of Phoenix, which opened its doors in 1976 and began offering online classes in 1989.

• The embrace of online teaching by traditional colleges and universities where, as described in a 2011 report by the Pew Internet and American Life Project (which incorporates survey research involving college presidents and students): "More than three-quarters of the nation's colleges and universities now offer online classes, according to the survey of college presidents, and about one-in-four college graduates (23%) have taken a course online, according to the general public survey. Among those who have graduated in the past decade, the figure rises to 46%."[9]

Experimentation

The Internet did not remain static as educators tried to figure out how to make use of its benefits while avoiding its pitfalls. Upsides of the new communications medium included dramatic increases in efficiency and rapid expansion of reach, while downsides included a developing culture of distraction that threatened to disrupt class time, not to mention a culture of giving things—including educational content—away for free that threatened to disrupt the business models undergirding higher education.

The emergence of social media products such as Facebook and Twitter provided the means to instantly create online communities, including communities of learners, who could participate in projects together regardless of geographical location. And as free, cloud-based resources tore down barriers to content creation and distribution, comparisons began to be drawn between the education field and newspapers and magazines that were not able to reinvent themselves quickly enough to avoid decimation by an online revolution in media.

Discussion of the educational potential of these tools was taking place within a wider decades-long and fretful conversation over an education system claimed to be in a perpetual state of crisis, even as proponents of pedagogical and political solutions were providing competing answers to less-than-clearly understood questions. This environment created a ready audience for anyone proposing technology-based cures (including magic bullets) for the ills of education, an audience that included parents staring down six-figure tuition bills that might buy their kids access to schools delivering ever-larger classes taught by adjuncts and graduate students rather than full professors.

Educational entrepreneurs and altruists, including countless emerging educational technology (or EdTech) ventures and educational nonprofits, were more than ready to provide their own alternatives in the form of educational products and programs, many of them leveraging the same all-but-free Internet infrastructure being used by large educational publishers and universities themselves to deliver a variety of proposed solutions to society's educational ills.

One of these ills was the aforementioned ever-increasing size of classes, a problem that could theoretically be solved by allowing small online communities of learners to band together based on their interests and ability level to create more intimate educational experiences tailored to the needs of individual students. But it would take until 2008 before one of these experimenters decided to deliberately *increase* class size as a means for improving education. And once the threshold of a thousand students in a single class was breached, the age of the MOOC had begun.

Opening Up the Class

Before "massiveness" became the focus of attention in online learning, "open" was the key driver for a series of experiments in online education from which today's MOOCs ultimately emerged.

As mentioned in chapter 1, the Massachusetts Institute of Technology's OpenCourseWare (OCW) initiative was founded in 2002 to make content from MIT's classroom-based courses available over the Internet to teachers, college students, and independent learners. Today, material from over 2,000 MIT classes, cutting across all disciplines, can be accessed and used for educational purposes, and MIT is a member of an OpenCourseWare Consortium that makes available multilingual educational materials from countries around the world.

OpenCourseWare provides a powerful example of how institutions can share educational resources with the public. However, the contents of OCW libraries can vary considerably from institution to institution and even from course to course. For example, only a small percentage of MIT's OCW classes include video recordings of lectures, with the majority of courses covered by lecture notes and slides alongside reading lists, exams, and other text-based content. And while anyone is free to follow along with a course syllabus (also provided for each course in the MIT OCW library), OpenCourseWare is generally not considered to provide a comprehensive substitute for structured MIT classes.

Throwing open the doors of existing structured classes to people not associated with the institution where

Before "massiveness" became the focus of attention in online learning, "open" was the key driver for a series of experiments in online education from which today's MOOCs ultimately emerged.

the course was being taught was a logical next step in the evolution of online openness.

Technology-wise, there was little to prevent course content that was already automated and delivered to students on and off campus through a school's online learning management system from being made available to people not connected with the college or university. But actually inviting the public to take a course for free (where they would be working alongside traditional students who had paid to take the same class) was a radical step taken by educational envelope pushers like Dr. David Wiley of Utah State University.[10]

In 2008, Wiley opened up one of his education courses to the world, allowing anyone interested to participate alongside his tuition-paying Utah State students. These external students were asked to take part in all of the class work performed by Utah students, including submitting written assignments that Dr. Wiley graded like any other papers submitted in his classes. And while Utah State did not provide official recognition or credit to external students taking the course for free, Dr. Wiley issued his own signed certificates of completion—prefiguring the types of quasi-official course-gradation documents that would come to characterize the MOOC reward system a few years later.

Now Wiley's experiment drew fewer than ten external enrollees who took the course alongside fifteen Utah State students, so grading papers and personally signing certificates represented a modest increase in workload, well worth the effort for a professor dedicated to evangelizing the benefits of open learning. But while that small Utah class was creating an important precedent for future open online course initiatives, further North another experiment would add massiveness into the equation.

The first course to earn the title of a MOOC was Connectivism and Connective Knowledge taught by Stephen Downes, senior researcher for the National Research Council of Canada, and George Siemens, associate director for the Technology Enhanced Knowledge Research Institute at Canada's Athabasca University.[11]

This 2008 course (which was repeated in 2011 and 2012) looks very different from the institution-based MOOC classes that would be making news from 2011 onward. For the connectivist approach to knowledge and learning that was the subject of the course also characterized the way the entire project was organized.

The connectivism model championed by pioneers such as Siemens and Downes sees knowledge and learning through the lens of how information becomes incorporated into the brain, an organic system in which billions of neurons form trillions of connections with learning measured in the net number of new connections created. Such a vision has obvious analogs with computer networks (which is why classes organized along connectivist principles are often referred to as "networked learning").

And once the Internet became large enough to facilitate a number of nodes that could be measured in the hundreds of millions (if not billions), it became possible to create a course based on this connectivist understanding of how people learn.

Unlike a standard online class delivering traditional classroom elements such as lectures, reading assignments, homework, and tests via a learning management system, Connectivism and Connective Knowledge was built around a variety of online communication tools with students forming organic communities through bulletin boards and chat rooms, social media products like Facebook and Twitter, or sharing services like RSS. And as these communities formed, they linked up with other communities as the network defining the class grew and evolved.

In order to provide some connective tissue for the program, Downes and Siemans posted a daily newsletter containing links to recommended articles, videos, and other content that students were free to review, discuss, add to, or ignore. And instead of attending scheduled lectures where the professors acted as sages performing from a virtual stage, students were invited to participate in biweekly presentations by the course leaders, by people the professors invited to speak, or by individuals drawn from the community of networked learners.

Under this connectivist framework, all material generated by the professors (such as presentations, reading recommendations, and discussion forums) was optional, with students free to use what they liked, create and share their own curriculum materials, and take the community-based conversation in directions never planned by the creators of the course.

Given this framework, large class size, assumed to be inversely proportional to teaching and learning quality in a traditional classroom setting, suddenly became an *asset* rather than a liability. For the bigger the connectivist "class," the greater the potential for the quantity and variety of nodal connections that define success for networked learning.

The term "MOOC" was created by another Canadian, David Cormier, manager of web communications and innovations at the University of Prince Edward Island and the host of the weekly EdTechTalk webcast. Cormier helped facilitate Downes's and Seimens's connective learning project and coined the term "Massive Open Online Course" or "MOOC" during an EdTechTalk interview with the course creators in 2008.[12]

The connectivist vision continues to generate a great deal of passion as well as a roster of online courses organized around its principles of decentralized networks. But as class sizes for these types of courses stabilized in the three- and four-figure range, a new vision for the MOOC—the xMOOC—would start racking up enrollments of tens and even hundreds of thousands.

xMOOC vs. cMOOC

The origin of what we now consider to be mainstream MOOCs, which began with the Stanford open learning experiment and evolved into consortia of colleges and universities delivering online courses through companies such as Coursera, Udacity, and edX, was described in chapter 1. But while such classes may have become synonymous with the term "MOOC" in the educational and popular media, people involved with some of the earlier experiments in online learning described in this chapter use the term xMOOC to distinguish the newer massive courses from the connectivist MOOCs (now referred to as cMOOCs) that came before.

Given that one of the saving graces of the otherwise unattractive MOOC acronym is its pronounceability, it's no surprise that this pair of unwieldy variants failed to capture an audience beyond a small community of learning specialists. And while it's tempting to characterize xMOOCs and cMOOCs as representing opposing pedagogies or ideologies with regard to their approach to large-scale online learning, such reductivism threatens to blur more interesting distinctions and overlaps between the two ways MOOCs have manifested themselves to date.

After all, "xMOOC" is not a banner the current crop of MOOCs from companies like Coursera and edX chose to travel under but rather is a label assigned to later forms of

MOOC classes by advocates for specific theories of connectivism. And unlike cMOOCs, xMOOCs are not built around a specific educational theory or pedagogy, even if most of them can be characterized as replicating traditional classroom models designed around lectures, homework assignments, and assessments.

Also, as interesting as connectivist educational models might be, and as important as cMOOCs were in breaking down barriers to large-scale online classes, the number of people who have chosen to participate in xMOOC classes surpasses cMOOC participants by at least two orders of magnitude. Now it is not at all clear whether the popularity of an MIT xMOOC like Circuits and Electronics (with enrollment of over 150,000) is due to its xMOOC nature, the subject matter, or the fact that it is a free course from MIT. But it does seem as though the emerging MOOC market is driven more by content and association with prestige universities than it is by either technology or pedagogical theory.

Regarding overlap between various flavors of MOOC, keep in mind the experimental nature of the entire massive open course undertaking, a culture of research, assimilation, and trial-and-error described in detail in chapter 5. So, far from seeing cMOOC experiments in community formation as a rival pedagogy, many creators of xMOOCs see classes like Connectivism and Connective Knowledge as just one more set of precedents to draw from as they put together and continued to tinker with their own massive online courses.

Family Tree

Rather than focusing on narrow x- and c-genera of the MOOC phenomenon, a better way to think about MOOC variants is by placing them on different branches of a far larger and more complex family tree alongside multiple variants of online learning, not to mention other modern teaching tools and techniques, all descending from a common pair of ancestors: technology and education.

With these two playing the role of Adam and Eve, descendants of the pairing of education and technology include not just multiple species of online education (which includes MOOCs, online colleges, and LMS-driven online learning within K–12 and higher education) but a host of transformations within the classroom where teachers at all grade levels are drawing upon new technology-based resources to construct, enliven, and transform how learning takes place, implementing pedagogies quite at odds with the way education has traditionally been delivered.

For instance, "Flipped Classroom Models"[13] involve replacing the usual sequence of in-class lectures followed by assignments and projects done at home with a new workflow that involves students watching recorded lectures as homework, freeing class time for extended in-depth discussion or work on complex individual and group projects. MOOCs are frequently brought up in discussions of flipping the class where it is assumed that recorded MOOC lectures will provide at-home video content. But even before the advent of MOOCs, educators have been implementing this method of teaching by recording their own lectures or curating material from different commercial and noncommercial third-parties for both homework/lectures and in-classroom exercises.

The concept of "curation," which involves teachers locating and procuring educational material from various sources and integrating it into the class, has also destabilized another mainstay of primary, secondary, and post-secondary education: the textbook. Whereas public school districts once purchased individual texts for each student (or, as in my own kids' schools, purchases two copies per student freeing them from having to drag heavy hardcover tomes home each day), they are now gravitating toward e-book versions of the same texts which are being supplemented by material found from sources like the open web.

Professors at colleges and universities who face less pressure than do K–12 teachers to use teaching resources—notably textbooks—selected for them (often based on compliance with state standards) have gone much further in replacing textbooks entirely with articles and other content pulled together into inexpensive custom coursepacks or delivered to students free through learning management systems or a library reserve service.

This move away from printed texts in both K–12 and higher education has led to changes across the educational economy, especially since the billions in textbook spending at the K–12 and college levels means that more educational dollars are tied up in this component of the education process than almost any other, including spending on school technology infrastructure. Expectations that this money would eventually find a new home fueled massive consolidation and acquisition activity within the textbook industry in the late 1990s and early 2000s as investors bet that established publishers would have the resources and customer base needed to take best advantage of a "move to digital" represented by the merging of content and technology. But as those textbook behemoths struggled to wean themselves off high-margin book sales and find and implement new business models that stood the risk of cannibalizing existing businesses, another set of investors started placing bets on younger, smaller high-tech startups that could offer new educational products and services unencumbered by existing high-profit product lines, legacy technology, or outmoded business practices. And some of the beneficiaries of this investor interest (some would say speculation) in EdTech have been MOOC companies that have received tens of millions of dollars in funding in the belief that millions of "eyeballs" obtained through giving college courses away for free could eventually be converted into revenue.

Before leaving the subject of textbooks, it should also be noted that one of the factors that left educational publishers open to customer flight was pricing policies that raised textbook prices at nearly twice the rate of inflation. While this also left publishers open to criticism and even political condemnation, these for-profit companies seemed a convenient surrogate for an attack on colleges and universities, whose costs were also spiraling beyond the reach of ordinary people leading to, among other problems, a trillion-dollar educational debt bubble that looms as the next great financial crisis.

While an analysis of the factors behind the exorbitant costs of college is beyond the scope of this book,[14] it should be noted that much of the discussion of MOOCs as a potential substitute for a traditional college education grows out of concerns that colleges and universities are pricing themselves out of a market and will need to be replaced (or at least supplemented) with different, less-expensive alternatives, alternatives that have the potential to disrupt the status quo.

As you can see from this history, the MOOC phenomenon is interwoven with and playing out against a backdrop of economics and politics, changes in educational pedagogies and approaches, and shifting expectations with regard to education resulting from the expanding capabilities and choices offered to students and teachers through new technologies.

In chapter 4 we will take a closer look at some of the issues that have grown out of the debate over massive open online courses. But before looking at such controversies, we need to answer a more fundamental question of what is (and just as important what is not) a MOOC?

WHAT MAKES A MOOC?

For anyone who has taken a massive online class from one of the major MOOC providers, the answer to the question of what constitutes a MOOC might seem obvious: the same lectures, reading and homework assignments, assessments, and discussions you would find in a traditional college class, albeit delivered in a digital format to thousands rather than live to dozens.

But, as I learned while taking dozens of such courses, when the content of a class moves from live to digital with the assumption that this material will be consumed by tens of thousands of students of differing and unknown abilities (including familiarity with the language in which the class is taught) working in widely ranging environments, not only do the elements of learning take on different attributes but the rules that define meaning when these elements are linked together in a traditional classroom may no longer apply.

To take one example, the seemingly simple decision of putting a MOOC on a calendar rather than making the same course available on demand (allowing students to start whenever they like with no fixed deadlines for completion) radically changes the nature of discussion in an online class, transforming it from a forum for working through ideas the class is grappling with week after week to an archive of insights primarily used to help students work through homework and assessments.

And then there is the question of what you earn upon completion of a MOOC vs. some other online learning experience. An online course that is part of an accredited degree program provides you actual credit hours you can apply toward a diploma, while an e-learning course in the latest version of Microsoft Office might earn you nothing more than some sort of informal certificate of mastery. MOOCs, on the other hand, generally provide those who complete a course with a certificate bearing the name of a prestigious institution. With some effort (described in the next chapter), certain MOOCs can be turned into college credit. But even if a massive course is taken purely for the sake of learning, the perceived value of a MOOC certificate can be higher than what you obtain by completing some garden-variety computer-based learning class, provided a student can figure out how to signal the value of their accomplishment to the wider world.

In this chapter, we take a look at all of the parts of a course and how they fit together in order to answer the question of what constitutes a MOOC. And in an era when e-learning providers are repackaging and rebranding their material as MOOC classes, we will also use this analysis to determine what might fall outside the category of a massive open online course.

Lectures

In many ways, the lecture is the most valuable component of any class in that it provides an expert (the instructor) an efficient means to deliver his or her expertise, built over years of teaching and researching a subject.

It has become fashionable to denigrate online classes, including most MOOCs, as simply taking "sage on the stage" lecturing that's been the cornerstone of education for centuries and moving it onto the screen. And while it is true that the lecture is an information transfer technique that has been the focal point of education (especially higher education) for centuries, there is a difference between maintaining a tradition out of inertia and sticking with a teaching strategy that works.

So are lectures an anachronism or a tool that, like a hammer, leave minimal room for dramatic improvement?

One of the most widely read books on the subject of lecturing is Donald Bligh's *What's the Use of Lectures?*[1] This work synthesized existing research on the efficacy of lecturing and came to the conclusion that of the four things teachers claim students should be getting from their lessons (the acquisition of information, promotion of thought, changes in attitude, and development of behavior skills), information acquisition is the only objective where data demonstrate the effectiveness of the lecture format.

This would help to explain why lecturing tends to predominate in higher education rather than in earlier grades. For earlier schooling must include large components of cognitive and behavior training, requiring early-grade classes to include forms of classroom exercises and interactions less necessary in higher education courses that focus more on information transfer.

Bligh makes it a point to acknowledge that while research based on evidence of performance might demonstrate important general principles regarding the effectiveness of the lecture format, statistics in themselves cannot capture specific instances of inspiring teachers able to use their lectures to do more than simply transfer knowledge. In the MOOC world, such teachers are often referred to as "rock star professors," implying that educators most attracted to teaching a massive online course are the ones whose mastery of the art of lecturing allows them to transcend limitations of the lecture format.

While characteristics such as a lecturer's "artistry" and "inspiration" (never mind "rock star" status) are difficult to quantify, one conclusion in Bligh's work—which jibes with more current research-based opinion regarding lecture length[2]—is that widely varying student attention spans and memory stamina point to the efficacy of shorter vs. longer lectures. (Bligh recommends 20–30 minutes vs. the traditional 1–2 hours of traditional college lectures.)

And with a few exceptions, MOOC developers have taken to heart the importance of breaking lecture material into shorter segments. Most of the massive classes I took through edX and Coursera, for example, "chunked" lectures (which tend to total between 1 and 3 hours of video per week) into 5–15 minute increments, while my classes from the early MOOC pioneer Udacity subdivided lectures into even tinier segments, most less than two minutes in length.

The fact that lectures are recorded also gives students access to video-player controls that allow them to speed up a professor they feel is taking too long to get to a point or back up to relisten to a point that might have been delivered too rapidly, giving students far more control over the rate of information transfer and acquisition than they would have in a live classroom. And while such controls are no more "high tech" than what VHS players allowed us to do thirty years ago, the ability to change speed, repeat, or skip microlectures has a pedagogical impact. For instance, students already knowledgeable about certain topics taught in a course can speed through or even skip videos on those subjects, while struggling students can repeat a lecture or return to it later, something that happens frequently during homework and assessment sequences. Speed controls and subtitling also support students with special needs or learners for whom English (still the primary language for MOOCs) is not their mother tongue.

Many of these controls have been standard in conventional online learning systems featuring video content, but MOOC developers often have access to things traditional online courses creators lack, such as production facilities and budgets that allow them to shoot on location or supplement "sage-on-stage" talking with interviews and recorded conversations, techniques that are beginning to create a new visual language associated with MOOC learning.

To cite a few examples, Harvard professor David Cox, who teaches an edX MOOC on neuroscience, has made it a point to get out of the building by visiting labs, hospitals, and other facilities where neuroscience research is taking place. And Udacity's Introduction to Psychology includes interviews with experts in animal behavior, sex and gender, and the facial expression of emotions, as well as skits and other types of creative performances.

Levels of creativity, not to mention production quality, continue to range widely across MOOC courses from different universities. For example, during a year when I took over thirty online classes, I observed a fair share of lighting- and audio-challenged lecture videos, as well as continuity errors (such as a professor's clothes changing and his beard appearing and disappearing within the same video segment) coupled with "outside the classroom" segments that were clearly repurposed student video projects. But I also observed attempts to use lectures to generate the sense of intimacy lacking in other components of a heavily subscribed MOOC.

As an example, for over thirty years Professor Greg Nagy has used a traditional lecture format to teach a course entitled The Ancient Greek Hero to both Harvard undergraduates and to adults via the Harvard Extension School, making Greek Hero one of the oldest continually running courses at that institution. But when it came time to turn that course into a MOOC, Nagy and the HarvardX production team replaced sage-on-stage lecturing with a series of conversations between the professor, his students, and his colleagues, giving MOOC students such as me the sense that we were in the room eavesdropping on intimate and passionate discussions between experts instead of sitting in a lecture hall being talked at by a single distant professor.

As new techniques for delivering lecture-style content continue to evolve within the framework of the overall MOOC experiment, we should not lose sight of the observation made earlier that some teachers, whether they be called "rock stars" or just highly gifted educators, have so mastered the artistry of lecturing that they would be successful in any modality of instruction. Ethics professor Michael Sandel, for example, teaches an overflow crowd of Harvard undergraduates whenever his popular Justice course is taught and teaches the same material before even larger groups when he takes his course on the road to eager audiences around the world. At the same time, recorded versions of his lectures were aired on public television and have been staples at iTunes U and YouTube for years, with those recordings also used to anchor an edX version of his course, which attracted over 60,000 students.

So while technical and production-level creativity and experimentation are some of the most exciting things to come out of investments being made in massive open learning, success or failure of the lecture—still the primary means by which information is transmitted to the student—usually comes down to the very traditional question of whether the teacher at the center of the course has the talent, skill, and flexibility to pull the whole thing off.

Reading

While there is evidence of written educational material going back to ancient times, and language primers (as well as other texts used to support rote learning) were available both before and after the advent of the printing press, textbooks that package content from diverse source[ ] [into a] single volume that can serve as the basis for a semes[ter- or] year-long class emerged in the eighteenth and ninet[eenth] centuries, when the teaching models that underlay our current educational system were being built.[3] But as those models begin to change and technology makes print an increasingly smaller subset of what we refer to as "publishing," there has been a broadening of what constitutes the reading associated with a course.

For instance, while college level classes in math and science subjects where material builds logically from one lesson to another still tend to rely on textbooks that present those building blocks with a common voice, professors teaching classes in the humanities and social sciences have traditionally required students to read a variety of material from different sources. In some cases (such as a Shakespeare class) the material students will read over a semester can still be consolidated into a single book. But for the most part such courses require students to obtain a collection of primary and secondary sources that make up the reading assignments for a class.

Even before technology enabled low-cost electronic distribution of content, however, students were not required to purchase everything they would read for a class from the bookstore. For instance, in cases where an article or excerpt from a longer text was assigned as required reading, students have historically obtained this material

So while technical and production-level creativity and experimentation are some of the most exciting things to come out of investments being made in massive open learning, success or failure of the lecture—still the primary means by which information is transmitted to the student—usually comes down to the very traditional question of whether the teacher at the center of the course has the talent, skill, and flexibility to pull the whole thing off.

from document databases or reserve room services offered through a college library, highlighting the criticality of the academic library with regard to the safe and legal distribution of academic content. For in addition to providing secure access to texts, including rare and valuable documents, libraries have also been given rights to distribute copyrighted material in a controlled manner that allows library personnel flexibility not available to others in the academy, including professors and students.

In our digital age, a hot issue in education and library science has to do with how far legal principles designed for a hard-copy era, when documents were doled out in a physical location where activities such as photocopying could be controlled, still apply when that same material can be made available electronically to students who, in addition to reading it as part of a class, can copy and paste (i.e., make illegal duplicates) of library-licensed, copyrighted material in the privacy of their own dorm rooms.

In the case of MOOCs, these intellectual property issues are compounded by the fact that students enrolled in most MOOC classes normally do not attend the college or university where the course originates, meaning that institution-specific database-licensing arrangements and legal doctrines related to reserve reading do not necessarily apply to the bulk of enrollees.

The other issue MOOC creators have had to contend with regarding adding required reading to a massive open online course has to do with the notion of "openness." Like intellectual property rules, the subject of open educational resources will be analyzed further in chapter 4, but for purposes of this discussion of reading, MOOCs are considered to be "open" to the extent that they are offered for free. And if a free MOOC class includes required reading that students would have to pay to obtain, how open (or democratic) can a MOOC program really be?

Early MOOCs dealt with this issue by eliminating reading lists entirely or by making syllabus reading optional rather than required. While this worked (and continues to work) for some courses, such strategies serve to increase the distance between MOOC learning and a more comprehensive educational experience that takes place in a traditional college classroom.

As more MOOCs come to market, professors have been experimenting with different methods to make required reading part of their courses in ways that do not leave institutions vulnerable to copyright-related lawsuits or create out-of-pocket expenses for students. Providing links to public domain or open access[4] educational content continues to be a popular strategy, most easily applied in courses where reading material is already publically available in legal, free formats. But this method still leaves gaps, illustrated by my reading experience in The Modern and the Postmodern, a popular Coursera MOOC on modern intellectual history taught by Professor Michael Roth, president of Wesleyan University. During the first half of the course, which focused on eighteenth and nineteenth-century philosophers and authors, those of us enrolled in the class were provided links to public domain versions of complete essays by writers such as Kant and Rousseau. But as the class continued on to twentieth- and twenty-first-century thinkers, those links started pointing us toward YouTube interviews and other public, secondary content, rather than contemporary, primary (and copyrighted) work.

Owners of protected material are beginning to come to terms with the unique requirements (and opportunities) related to MOOCs being taken by tens of thousands of students. For example, Greg Nagy—the professor behind the HarvardX Ancient Greek Hero course mentioned earlier—gave up royalties to a textbook he had written in exchange for making the content of the book available to all MOOC subscribers for free. And as the MOOC phenomenon gained momentum in 2013, traditional textbook publishers began their own business-model experiments by offering students time-limited electronic editions of otherwise expensive textbooks at no cost during the length of a course, then providing them the option to buy the book at a discount after the course had been completed.[5]

As institutions become more adept at navigating intellectual property rules and professors more experienced in leveraging open resources, new strategies for including robust reading requirements in a massive online course will continue to develop. At the same time, exposure to a wider variety of resources and strategies related to syllabus reading is also providing professors new perspectives that have helped them rethink the role reading plays in their traditional classroom-based courses.

Separate from all of these issues related to sourcing reading content are continuing concerns over whether students are being assigned enough reading or are actually doing the reading assigned to them in college classes, whether that reading is delivered as a textbook or custom course pack (either printed or online) or as a list of links to individual pieces of content. Reading is one of the many subjects discussed in the 2011 book *Academically Adrift,*[6] which challenges higher education claims of rigor as it applies across all academic activities at traditional college campuses. So while information on completion of reading assignments within MOOCs does not yet exist, issues regarding this largely unmonitored course component transcend teaching modality. But given the self-motivation required to complete a massive open online course successfully, it may turn out that commitment to reading is the differentiator between those who succeed in MOOCs and other experiments in alternative learning and those who get nothing out of them.

Discussion and Community

The advantages and disadvantages of online vs. live class-room discussion have been argued over since the advent of technology-based distance education.[7,8] Even when online discussion was implemented primarily through bulletin-board-style commenting systems that today's social-media-savvy students would find primitive, supporters pointed out that such systems gave students the opportunity to gather their ideas and respond thoughtfully to a teacher's questions, as well as allow students to reply to one another's postings—opening up the opportunity for students teaching students. Supporters also highlighted that online commenting systems give teachers the ability to enforce and monitor student interchange as well as provide those who might be hesitant to speak in a group the opportunity to participate in discussion without the social pressures present in the classroom. But critics argued that online discussion boards could never support the type of give-and-take achievable in the live classroom or small discussion group (never mind the all-night dorm room bull session) where genuine conversation, including the facial and body language that makes up so much of human communication, is a natural part of face-to-face interchange.

The original bulletin-board-style commenting systems still prevalent in most online courses are an example of *asynchronous communication,* in which interchanges between students and teachers or students and students are not immediate but rather spread out over time (much like the commenting systems that allow readers to provide feedback to stories posted on online news sites). But in the two decades since online education came on the scene, new Internet-based communication tools such as Skype, Google Hangouts, and other audio and video conferencing services—some of them built directly into learning management systems—have allowed teachers and students to participate in *synchronous communication* activities, replicating live classes or discussion sections at a distance.

Some of these services have been incorporated into popular social media systems like Facebook and Google+, which allow instructors to create social network sites associated with a class as well as give students the opportunity to create their own communities to facilitate discussion or joint work on a class project. And as professors make blogs and social networking tools a component of traditional classroom-based courses (asking every student to create a weekly posting on a class blog as a homework assignment, for example), the distinction between live-classroom vs. online learning has become increasingly blurry.

Unlike other forms of student engagement that must be measured indirectly (through tools such as self-report surveys or assessments of comprehension), online discussions leave the type of data trail beloved by educational researchers. For instance, a study by the Silicon Valley company Piazza, whose software powers discussion functionality for over 10,000 classes, looked at the online behavior of students in 3,600 courses from over 500 institutions over 18 months to see what trends emerged.[9] The research included some interesting findings, such as the observation that mandatory commenting seems to correlate with comment volume, but not necessarily with student comprehension. As anecdotal responses to a *Chronicle of Higher Education* story on this research (submitted, it should be noted, via an online commenting system) pointed out, however, the effectiveness of online discussion can vary enormously based on variables such as the nature of the class (100 percent online, classroom-based, or hybrid), class size, and the comfort level of teachers and students with the chosen communication technologies.

Given that MOOCs tend to attract teachers and students confident in their use of technology-based education tools, challenges regarding discussion and community formation within MOOCs derive not from the technological adeptness of users but rather from the sheer size of the community being asked to participate in discussion.

In the next chapter, we will take a closer look at those five- and six-figure MOOC enrollment numbers to see what they are really telling us about participation and attrition rates. But even if we assume that only the 5 to 15 percent of enrollees who tend to complete a massive online course are also participating in discussion forums, this still makes MOOC-based discussion communities significantly larger (sometimes by an order of magnitude) than similar communities in even the biggest traditional online courses.

Drawing again from courses I completed during my one-year BA experiment, the general comments section for Professor Michael Roth's Coursera class The Modern and the Postmodern alone included 468 unique threads that drew 4,315 comments viewed over 75,000 times. And given that this general category represented approximately half the total comments generated for the course (other comments fell into categories such as study groups, assignments, and technical feedback), the volume of discussion taking place in online forums led some students to complain of feeling overwhelmed.

Highlighting this issue of overcrowding still further, the aforementioned HarvardX Justice class taught by Professor Michael Sandel required students to submit at least two comments in response to prompts associated with each week's assignments. This requirement led to weekly postings of thousands of student replies to the same questions, with each reply constituting a new forum discussion thread. In theory, students were free to reply to one another's postings as well as vote each other's comments up or down, with the expectation that this would cause the most thoughtful submissions to rise to the top of favorability rankings. But given the huge number of threads all related to the same topics, only a tiny percentage of posts received replies of any sort. And as for voting, less than 1 percent of comments earned even one or two votes, with only a handful receiving more than ten, indicating that the vast majority of forum participants (including me) were largely talking to themselves.

MOOC developers have tried a number of methods to supplement message boards with other strategies to support community formation among enrollees in massive online classes. For example, most courses kick off with a forum devoted to letting students find one another based on geographic proximity or commonalities in language or interest, with links providing students further information about existing course-specific "meet-ups" in their area. While these tools are meant to help those enrolled in classes find each other so that they can form real-world study or discussion groups, the fact that MOOC students are so widely distributed around the world means such gatherings tend to get proposed only for high-density locations such as major cities. And even in those locations, most stories surrounding meet-up attempts involve students getting stood up or physical study groups petering out after a few meetings.[10]

This does not prevent students from creating *online* communities, which tend to be most widespread in classes where students are required to organize into groups to work together on a common project. For example, an open class I took on entrepreneurship offered by Stanford University through the Novoed online learning platform asked students to form teams in order to perform research related to starting a new company based on the theories of startup planning and development taught in the course. But for the majority of MOOC classes that do not have such team exercises as a focus, community formation continues to be an ad-hoc process among independent MOOC participants.

Other communication techniques MOOC providers have used with varying degrees of success include online conferencing, where a small group of students are selected to interact directly with the professor, with the rest of the class allowed to eavesdrop on their conversation and submit their own questions via social media. Professors have also made occasional appearances in discussion forums, although having TAs help answer questions and guide conversation tends to be more common. It has also become increasingly popular for courses to add "office hour" videos to the weekly lecture lineup in which instructors address specific questions arising in the forums. Finally, MOOC vendors have recently been experimenting with programs like Coursera's "Learning Hubs" in which online courses are taught in a physical classroom where facilitators lead discussion and oversee work on class projects, combining the online learning experience with the traditional classroom model, much the same way MOOCs are being implemented in less developed countries where they are used to provide the lecture component for conventional high-school and college classes.

While there is a general consensus that MOOCs still need to find the means to create intimacy within classes taken by thousands of students, it should be noted that within existing MOOC communities (where more than half of class participants are college educated, many with advanced degrees), discussion levels can be quite high. For example, while studying Shakespeare's *Troilus and Cressida*, a play set during the Trojan War, I discovered an Achilles who bore little resemblance to the one we were reading about in my HarvardX Ancient Greek Hero MOOC. And when I posted an inquiry about this discrepancy in the HeroesX discussion forum, a fellow student provided a detailed historical analysis of the texts Shakespeare would have had available when writing the play. So while the interchanges in massive course forums occasionally degenerate into flame wars, more typical experiences involve students sharing their diverse expertise to facilitate some of the student-to-student teaching envisioned by the early MOOC pioneers described in chapter 2.

Even when these systems work, however, discussion is still an activity participated in by a small percentage of MOOC students—albeit the ones most likely to be committed to, and thus likely to succeed in, turning their classroom experience into genuine learning.

Assessment

Assessment can make an appearance in a number of places within a MOOC. For example, lecture videos are often punctuated with automatically scored questions (which usually don't contribute to an overall grade) that assess comprehension of information that has just been presented. Homework assignments, which may or may not contribute to a grade, often consist of short quizzes or activities requiring students to post the results of their work into a multiple-choice form. And final grades for most MOOC courses tend to be based on automatically scored exams, usually consisting of multiple-choice, matching, or fill-in-the-blank test items, and/or work products that are either self-graded or peer-graded based on a rubric supplied by the professor to student evaluators. All of these assessment techniques are created with the assumption that classes consisting of tens of thousands of students require evaluation to be performed by someone other than a professor and his or her teaching team, which is why most MOOC grading is done either by computers or class participants.

Computer-based assessment has been widely used in education for decades, with learning management systems such as Blackboard and Moodle offering modules for creating familiar item types such as multiple-choice, multiple-response (multiple-choice with more than one correct answer), true-false, fill-in-the-blank, and matching items.

These systems, as well as various standalone testing products, also support student submission of more complex work (called "artifacts") such as text-based short answers to questions, essays, or multimedia submissions that will ultimately be scored by a human grader. Advances in technology-delivered testing and grading have also included automated "first-pass" scoring of essays, performance-based testing in which students are graded on their ability to perform a function (such as using a feature of a software program correctly) rather than answering multiple-choice questions, and adaptive testing in which an assessment gets harder or easier based on how well students perform on individual test questions.[11]

On top of these advances in assessment delivery and scoring, educational publishers have been providing teachers access to large banks of test questions, usually associated with a particular textbook. And teachers, including those moving a class they have taught for years or even decades into a massive online environment, usually have stacks of assessments they have generated during that time to repurpose for use in a MOOC.

Given all of this technology and content to fall back on, it is surprising that (based on many years of experience I've had in the professional testing industry) assessment continues to be one of the weakest areas in many MOOCs, including those that have made significant investments in other portions of a course, such as quality video production.

Given all of this technology and content to fall back on, it is surprising that assessment continues to be one of the weakest areas in many MOOCs.

The core testing methodology used in most MOOCs is linear assessment consisting of automatically scored multiple-choice and similar test items. But while the creation of such test items supports an entire industry of professional test developers who use scientific principles of test planning and item design and analysis to create valid and reliable exams for educational accountability, college entrance, certification, and professional licensure, very few of the assessments associated with MOOCs demonstrate the involvement of professional test designers. The continued use in MOOC assessments of true/false questions—an item type eschewed by professional exam developers—testifies to the fact that exam creation in a MOOC is primarily based on using what course developers have at hand (often repurposed content from classroom versions of the course) rather than on the creation of more challenging assessments designed to effectively discriminate between those who have mastered the material and those who have not.

This general observation regarding assessment strength should not imply that every course lacks rigorous measurement of learning. For instance, courses I completed that covered subjects incorporating numerical information, such as math, science, or statistics, tended to feature stronger assessments simply because they include test questions requiring numerical input—including numbers derived from calculation or even experimentation—that are intrinsically more difficult to guess at than selecting an answer from a multiple-choice list would be.

While use of professional test design principles, coupled with some creativity, could dramatically improve the effectiveness of machine-scored assessments, MOOC developers have primarily looked at ways to grade subjective material, such as natural language short answers and essays, as a means to make their courses more challenging.

For instance, the edX version of the popular Harvard course Science and Cooking required participants to generate weekly write-ups of lab experiments students performed in their own kitchens with self-grading performed by the students themselves using scoring rubrics provided only after a student's work has been submitted.

While such self-grading has been applied in other courses, most rubric-scored assessment of subjective material within MOOCs is done via the mechanism of *peer grading*. This is a process whereby students submit an assigned piece of work, most frequently an essay, that then gets put into a pool and distributed to other students for scoring. Students submitting their own work are generally required to grade the work of classmates, which usually involves providing numeric scores along multiple rubric criteria as well as qualitative commentary on three to five other student essays. Those numeric results are then averaged to calculate a final grade, and students can see the scores associated with their own work, as well as student commentary, at the end of a grading period.

Some informal research that indicated a sizable correlation (88%) between how a professor would have graded assignments compared to the result of the peer-grading process described above[12] was used to bolster claims that peer grading is a reasonable option for basing MOOC scores on the evaluation of complex artifacts by the student body rather than a professor. But even if such gross correlation numbers turn out to hold across a wider variety of courses, the fact remains that creating assignments that need to be human scored by hundreds or thousands of untrained evaluators inevitably leads to the creation of essay questions and grading rubrics built around ease of scoring rather than complexity of assignment. And given the global nature of MOOCs, the language skill of students acting as both writers and evaluators plays an as-yet-unmeasured role in the peer-grading process, especially in cases where writing quality is one of the rubric-based scoring metrics.[13]

As with linear test development, professional test design principles provide insights that could inform the creation of better assignments associated with stronger rubrics as MOOCs continue to develop. For example, grading of subjective work (such as the essays that are part of SAT and ACT) makes use of "first-pass" automated essay scoring technology as well as methodologies designed to maximize inter-rater reliability (the consistency of scoring between different evaluators) through a combination of design principles and training that could be incorporated into the MOOC peer-grading process.[14]

One advantage of the traditional classroom is that it includes a single arbitrator (the teacher) who has ultimate say in grading decisions, something ultimately lacking in MOOC grading procedures that provide little or no room for appeal. To a large extent, MOOCs have avoided complaints (at least by students) by making it easy for anyone who puts genuine effort into a course to get a passing grade. Most MOOCs are pass/fail, for example, with cut scores in the 60 to 70 percent range, sometimes with higher grades of 80 to 95 percent leading to a certificate reflecting special distinction. And the fact that many courses allow students to take the same test more than once (sometimes as many as 100 times!) means students can guess their way to a passing grade, even if they have learned none of the material.

This highlights another set of reasons why testing seems to be given less attention in a MOOC than it would get in a traditional classroom environment. First off, there are security concerns (discussed further in the next chapter) based on the fact that, despite honor codes and some anticheating experiments by MOOC providers, there is still no way to ensure that the person submitting an assignment is the person who has done the work. And even if such work does originate from the student enrolled in the course, there is no way of telling what resources they had on hand when they took (or cheated on) an exam or wrote (or plagiarized) a writing assignment. This lack of security leads to the reasonable fear that harder testing might simply lead to more cheating rather than more learning. And then there is a tendency among many MOOC professors to want to keep as many students as possible from dropping out of a course before the last set of lectures, which may limit their interest in more numerous or challenging assignments that stand the chance of scaring students off.

The fact that no tangible reward is associated with passing a MOOC should mitigate cheating problems (at least until MOOCs start being associated with something of value—such as genuine college credit), and in the absence of such college equivalency, choices of course difficulty have been appropriately left in the hands of the professor. But by making tests, homework, and other assignments too easy (by design or just by lack of interest in significantly improving them), MOOC courses may be robbing students of the chance to put their learning to work, which can limit a course's overall effectiveness. So until challenging assessments designed to verify and reinforce learning become a higher priority, MOOCs may continue to be perceived as a lighter alternative to what currently takes place in the less massively enrolled physical classroom.

Organizing a Course

Like any course, a MOOC cannot be considered simply to be the sum of its parts—such as lectures, reading, discussion, and assignments/assessments—especially given the unique characteristics and requirements these components have in a massive learning environment. Rather, the way those parts are put together, especially with regard to decisions relating to time and level of rigor, has a significant impact on the nature of the student learning experience.

To take an extreme example, the connectivist cMOOCs described in chapter 2 are so different in their organizational structure and expectations compared to xMOOCs (which more resemble traditional college classes) that cMOOCs and xMOOCs are best seen as completely distinct learning experiences, even if both happen to support free education of large numbers of students.

Within the family of major MOOC providers, the majority of courses from companies such as edX and Coursera share a similar approach to scheduling, with courses put on a calendar in which students engage with the same material each week until a fixed deadline is reached, at which point all work is required to be submitted for final grading. This is in sharp contrast to "on demand" courses, such as those offered via the MOOC provider Udacity, in which students can start the course whenever they like and work through the lessons at their own pace, with no fixed deadline for completing the material.

Each of these two modes of course timing (scheduled vs. on-demand) has advantages and disadvantages. For instance, putting classes on a calendar tends to create a sense of urgency to complete coursework on time but at the cost of the kind of flexibility you get from on-demand classes. And once organizations such as Coursera and edX have more courses "in the can" and ready to repeat, there are no technical reasons for not offering on-demand options for some or all of their materials.

But the choice of timing strategy can dramatically affect the nature of a class, particularly with regard to discussion, given that scheduled classes can be built on the assumption that students will be interacting with the same material at the same time. Even with all the previously noted challenges intrinsic to high-volume discussion boards, the bulk of comments posted to forums associated with scheduled courses involve students discussing issues related to the week's course material. In contrast, I discovered that discussion for on-demand courses tends to focus on students supporting one another on tests and homework assignments with limited interchange on more general topics.

Testing is another area affected by whether or not a course is on a fixed schedule. For even with all the security challenges mentioned in the previous discussion of MOOC assessment, deadlines at least put an end to the relevance of a particular quiz or exam, in contrast to an on-demand course where the same test items might live on for much longer, leading to issues of question overexposure. Now the security advantage of scheduled courses is diminished if professors overseeing them do not choose to swap out their assessment items each time a course is given. But assessment is one more area where decisions regarding how a MOOC is chronologically structured can dramatically affect important elements of the course.

Another time-related choice MOOC developers get to make that can dramatically influence the nature of the student learning experience is the overall length of a course. For instance, courses I completed that attempt to cover all of the learning objectives found in an existing full-semester college course tended to mirror the 12- to 16-week length of a semester-long class. Developers of such courses also generally place more demands on students with regard to required reading, frequency and difficulty of assessment, assignment of peer-graded work, and/or requirements to participate in online discussion boards. In contrast, professors who want to focus on a specific set of topics, rather than replicate a full-semester experience, tend to gravitate toward creating shorter courses, with six to eight weeks becoming an increasingly popular format for class length. Unsurprisingly, classes that go on for one to two months, compared to three to four for full-semester classes, often have higher enrollments and lower attrition rates. But given that level of demand with regard to reading, homework, and assessment tends to be lower for short vs. long courses, MOOCs seem to be stratifying based on differing tiers of overall rigor.

Decisions on the nature of a course (such as length, level of demand, and pass/fail requirements) are ultimately made by professors based on the mission they choose for their courses. And given the modular nature of MOOC components, experimentation with MOOC courses of varying lengths and demand levels is both natural and liberating, preventing a one-size-fits-all model from gripping this new educational medium.[15]

All this variability needs to be taken into account when entering the fiery debate over whether or not MOOCs should be treated as the equivalent of traditional college courses. For as my year taking courses with widely ranging course timing and strategies suggests, by intention all MOOCs are NOT created equal.

Graduation/Credit

When Sebastian Thrun realized that the free online version of his Stanford Artificial Intelligence course was going to be taken by tens of thousands of students, the biggest challenge he faced was not technical or pedagogical but political: would he be allowed to associate the name of Stanford University with whatever documentation he ended up providing students who completed the class?[16]

Thrun and Stanford eventually came to an agreement that allowed the university's name to appear on a carefully worded certificate of completion stating explicitly that the online course should not be considered equivalent to an actual paid-for Stanford for-credit course. And with this compromise, a reward system that tapped the prestige of well-known institutions of higher learning without necessarily putting those institutions' economic interests at risk was ready to become the norm for MOOC graduates.

The next chapter looks at some of the economic issues related to what brick-and-mortar colleges are actually selling in an era when many of their courses can be taken for free. But as we reach the end of this discussion over what makes a MOOC, the significance of a completion document bearing the imprimatur of a well-known and respected college or university should not be minimized.

Today, students are free to enroll in an online university and spend money on courses that can ultimately turn into credit toward a degree with no ambiguity whatsoever regarding institutional support for a graduate's final diploma. And students also have a wide range of learning options to draw from, such as academic lectures from iTunes U or eLearning lessons from commercial entitles such as Lynda.com, that leave them with nothing at the end of a course other than, perhaps, a vendor-specific certificate of mastery that means little or nothing to important audiences like employers.

But MOOCs create an intriguing ambiguity in which colleges and universities are extolling their own contribution to free public learning, implying that earning a MOOC certificate of completion represents genuine academic accomplishment, while simultaneously not rewarding this accomplishment in the way they reward students who have studied the same material with the same teacher in a classroom or online format that is not a MOOC. This ambiguity is at the heart of many of the issues and controversies described in chapter 4. But before getting there, it is worth asking the question this chapter has been leading up to, namely, what is (and isn't) a MOOC?

What is a MOOC?

The MOOC acronym provides a tempting framework in which to determine if a course does or does not deserve this title. Is a course massive? Is it open and online? Then it must be a MOOC!

But upon reflection, what is the threshold for a course being "massive" rather than just really big? And what sort of activity constitutes a student being "enrolled" in any sort of large-scale public learning project?

For example, does an iTunes U course that's been downloaded by a million people count as a massive course compared to an edX class that draws just a fraction of that number? And, if not, what is missing? Do recorded lectures lack the kind of community that would form around students taking the same course at the same time? If so, why were courses from companies like Udacity automatically rewarded the title of MOOCs, even though their on-demand nature limits the formation of communities of simultaneous learners? Perhaps the problem is that recorded lectures lack components such as reading assignments and assessments, which makes them seem less than a MOOC. But most iTunes U courses are recordings of existing college classes with associated syllabi, which means there is nothing stopping students from locating and following along with a course reading list while they listen to downloaded lectures. And given that assessment is often one of the weakest elements of a MOOC package, why should an Ohio State University course on Life in the Universe delivered as 44 full-length lectures via iTunes be considered inferior to an eight-week Coursera class on the same subject just because the latter might include a few multiple-choice tests of questionable utility?

As previously mentioned, "open" in the context of massive open online courses tends to be interpreted by the public as "free" (free of costs and free of any other sort of entrance requirement). So perhaps a line can be drawn that says any course with no barriers to entry will be considered a MOOC and everything else just some other variant on eLearning. But even today, costs and restrictions are not unknown in courses that bear the MOOC label. For instance, while students may not be required to buy a book or piece of equipment to take part in a MOOC, there already exist classes in which making such purchases is necessary to get the maximum value out of the class.[17] There are also examples of MOOCs coming with prerequisites (albeit mostly unenforced), and at least one of the major MOOC vendors has placed enrollment limits on at least one experimental class.[18] In theory we could use that aforementioned line to separate courses with zero restrictions (which we would still call MOOCs) from any course of any size from any institution that includes any barrier to participation. But if the major MOOC vendors decided tomorrow that their survival depended on charging students a few dollars a month for access to all the same content, does that mean every course taught up that point would immediately transform from a MOOC to something not a MOOC?

If a definition based on dissecting the MOOC acronym seems to lead too easily to illogical conclusions, perhaps we should simply declare that only courses from Coursera, edX, and Udacity should be considered MOOCs, or that MOOCs can be created only by prestigious colleges and universities. But such a narrow definition would embalm a hierarchy that may no longer be in place by the time you are reading this book.[19] And if academic snobbery is going to be our guiding principle over which courses get named "MOOCs," who gets to decide which colleges and universities deserve to be considered "prestigious"?

Such restrictions seem especially bizarre in a field as dynamic as educational technology, with few barriers preventing new MOOC players emerging and forming partnerships with colleges and universities up and down the academic pecking order. For example, at the end of 2013, two new international MOOC providers, FutureLearn (an initiative of Britain's venerable Open University) and Germany's iversity, opened their virtual doors to deliver classes from several European universities. At the same time, learning management system (LMS) providers (notably Instructure with its Canvas.net MOOC course catalog) began to see what would happen if existing courses on their platform were opened up to the world. And what are we to make of Udemy, a venture-funded company that allows anyone to post a course online and charge whatever he or she likes for it (including nothing)? While it might seem easy to dismiss a platform in which a handful of relatively low-enrollment academic courses are offered alongside hundreds or thousands of fee-based classes in subjects such as Microsoft Office or yoga, what would happen if a major university decided to not wait in line to partner with one of the more well-known MOOC providers but instead started releasing quality content through this kind of open platform?[20]

If assignment of the "MOOC" label is to be left to something other than public perception based on hype and whim, we may need to stop thinking about MOOCs in terms of their characteristics (size, cost, features) and instead think about their purpose, which (drawing on the philosophy vocabulary I learned during my One Year BA) switches us from an *empirical* hunt for definition to a *teleological* one. And here is what some of the companies and individuals who created the MOOC movement have to say about what they brought into being:

> We are committed to research that will allow us to understand how students learn, how technology can transform learning, and the ways teachers teach on campus and beyond.[21]
>
> —edX

> [MOOCs have] the potential of giving us a completely unprecedented look into understanding human learning. Because the data we can collect here is unique. You can collect every click, every homework submission, every forum post, from tens of thousands of students. So you can turn the study of learning from a hypothesis-delivered mode to a data-delivered mode, a transformation that has, for

example, revolutionized biology. You can use these data to understand fundamental questions, like what are good learning strategies that are effective versus ones that are not.[22]

—Daphne Koller, cofounder of Coursera

There always has been research, but the way it developed over the years was in closed learning management systems, accessible only to instructors and students in an individual class which made it very difficult to experiment, very difficult to replicate. … That changes with open online learning and that really comes to the fore with MOOCs. … And when it's done in these open environments, it's no surprise at all that you would see a renaissance in research, in experimentation, in trying new things, and I think that's a great thing.[23]

—Stephen Downes

So while educational altruism has certainly been an inducement for colleges and universities to participate in one or more MOOC projects, a commitment to educational research and experimentation may end up providing the most important distinction between MOOCs and other forms of online learning. Using this purpose as a means of discerning what is a MOOC and what is not provides lee-way regarding what constitutes "massive" and "open" (and even a "course"). For as long as those behind a learning project that includes most (although not necessarily all) of the features described in this chapter also demonstrate a commitment to experimentation and evolution, a willingness to try new things, a readiness to reject (while not punishing) failure while building upon success, then they are participating in the spirit that can define the MOOC enterprise.

So with the components and definitional framework discussed in this chapter in mind, it is now time to take a look at some of the issues and controversies surrounding MOOCs in chapter 4, followed by a review of the type of experimentation at the heart of the MOOC project in chapter 5.

ISSUES AND CONTROVERSIES

The transition from a period of exuberance over the potential for MOOCs (corresponding to Gartner's Hype Cycle "Peak of Inflated Expectations" described in chapter 1) to a "Trough of Disillusionment" was marked by a series of controversies within the academy driven largely by educators concerned that serious questions regarding academic quality and rigor were being ignored by the engineers, administrators, and policymakers who were excitedly hailing MOOCs as a solution to problems ranging from class overcrowding and college affordability to global underdevelopment.

Such naysaying was first treated as the carping of Luddites,[1] which could be balanced by the enthusiasm of more tech-savvy professors participating in MOOC projects. As more people started taking actual massive courses and as more data generated from those MOOCs became available, however, it became clear that the concerns of critics could not simply be dismissed as complaints by resentful academics standing in the way of progress shouting "Stop!"

As mentioned in chapter 1, the seemingly straightforward decision of Amherst College to take a wait-and-see approach to participating in MOOC development in April 2013 served as notice that not all colleges and universities wanted to be part of the mad scramble to join one of the consortia forming around companies like Coursera and edX. And when members of the philosophy department of San Jose State University revolted against a decision by their administration to license content from edX (also described in chapter 1), their protest set the stage for an academic backlash that continued in both the academic and popular press.

Complaints lodged by educators regarding this new huge-scale form of learning focused on the efficacy of an educational format where information was delivered by video lecture and measurement performed largely through multiple-choice quizzing, with student-to-student interaction facilitated by overcrowded discussion boards and student-to-teacher interaction virtually nonexistent. Were MOOC students really being asked to do the same level of work and getting the same level of education as their counterparts taking courses covering comparable material in traditional classroom environments? How was anyone supposed to know who was doing the work diligently and honestly and who was cheating his or her way to a passing grade? Who was actually enrolling in these courses and why were they choosing to participate? And, speaking of enrollments and participation, why should anyone have faith in an academic program with drop-out rates topping 90 percent?

Like the claims made by early MOOC enthusiasts, accusations hurled by critics were higher on emotion and third-party anecdotes than on data and first-person experience. But with more data available and more real-world experience to draw on, we are now in a better position to answer the serious and legitimate questions that continue to hover over the MOOC experiment.

Drop-Out Rates

One of the most damning indictments directed at MOOCs has to do with their seemingly huge rates of attrition. "Although they are rarely mentioned by MOOC supporters, drop-out rates in these courses hover at about 90 percent," noted Susan Meisenhelder, professor emeritus of English at California State University, San Bernardino, in a harsh critique entitled "MOOC Mania" in the Fall 2013 issue of the NEA higher education journal *Thought & Action*.[2] But by the time that piece was published, many of her concerns regarding massive online courses had largely gone mainstream. More important, enough data were available to paint a more accurate and nuanced picture of the life cycle of students participating in MOOC classes.

To set the stage for a more detailed analysis, the calculation used to determine drop-out rates in the range of 90 percent involves putting the number of students who sign up for a MOOC course (the source of those 100,000+ enrollment numbers that earned so much press attention) into the denominator of a fraction with the number of students who earn a certificate by completing a course serving as the numerator. Such a calculation, which treats every sign-up as the equivalent of a course enrollment decision by students attending a traditional college or university, does indeed translate to an attrition rate topping 90 percent for many MOOC courses.

But this opens up important questions about whether or not online sign-ups should be treated as representing the same level of commitment as enrolling in a traditional college course. Using an analogy from brick-and-mortar colleges and universities, many such schools feature "shop-around periods," which allow students to visit a few lectures early in the semester before committing to a schedule. And such shoppers, as well as auditors who sit in on lectures without taking the course for a grade, are reasonably excluded from any calculations regarding average grades and drop-out rates. But if a potential MOOC student curious about a course clicks on the Enroll button to get a closer look at the syllabus and course requirements or to size up the teacher they will be spending several weeks learning from, should this be considered the equivalent of formal enrollment in the class or would it be more comparable to "shopping" classes or even just browsing through a college catalog?

The online nature of MOOCs increases the likelihood that someone will hit an Enroll button before making a commitment to taking the course. MOOCs are free, after all, and the process for signing up for one involves little more than providing an e-mail address and password. And like sign-ups for social network sites such as Facebook or Google+, account creation does not translate into active participation. The fact that MOOCs are offering something of value (a college course) for free with no consequences for nonparticipation creates even more incentive to sign up for a class, regardless of whether or not students have thought through their plans regarding the course. With that in mind, does the huge denominator of the drop-out fraction mentioned above translate to large numbers of disillusioned students, or is it just an unsurprising big number that reflects people's willingness to fill out a brief online form in order to get something for nothing? But if the number of people hitting the Enroll button is not the best statistic to calculate actual participants in a MOOC class, what is?

Several studies performed by colleges and universities that have participated in MOOC projects provide a better understanding of what students are doing in a class beyond enrolling and either completing or not completing it. For example, the University of Edinburgh analyzed the results of six MOOCs they had delivered via Coursera starting in January 2013 on subjects in both the sciences and humanities.[3] And Professor Jeffrey Pomerantz, director of undergraduate studies at the School of Information and Library Science at the University of North Carolina in Chapel Hill, who taught the course Metadata: Organizing and Discovering Information (also delivered through Coursera), shared statistics related to participation with students in his class as well as publically documenting his analysis of activity, including completion rates, at the end of the course.[4]

Coursera's learning management system breaks student enrollment lists into "Total Registered Students" (the number of people who hit the Enroll button in order to sign up for a class who don't subsequently unenroll), "Total Active Students" (the number of unique students who logged into the site at least once after sign-up), and "Active Students Last Week" (the number of unique students who log into the system on a week-by-week basis).

In Pomerantz's Metadata course, for example, 27,623 people enrolled in the class (with that total enrollment number dropping to 25,867 as people unenrolled before the end of the eight-week class). The number of Total Active Students grew from 10,476 to 14,130 during this same period, while the number of weekly unique participants fell from 10,470 to 3,334.

These data, as well as other details about student participation in video lectures, discussion boards, and assignments, allowed Professor Pomerantz to calculate attrition rates based on different ways of defining an active student. For example, with 1,418 actual graduates (i.e., students who completed all the work and earned a certificate of completion), using total enrollment as the denominator for calculating a completion rate generates a completion percentage of 5 percent. And while using Total Active Students doubles that completion percentage, both calculations lead to the more than 90 percent drop-out rate highlighted by MOOC critics.

But if you assume that only students who actually do something on a course site rather than just log into it once are actually participating in the class, the numbers tell a different story. For example, the completion percentage for students who watch at least one lecture video was 15 percent in Pomerantz's Metadata class, while the percentage of students who had done the first homework exercise and then went on to finish the course was 48 percent.

The most systematic research on student behavior within MOOC classes comes from Harvard and MIT who released detailed analyses of student activity in 16 edX courses in January 2014. While this research will be discussed further in chapter 5, data from these studies also indicate that residential college enrollment and class participation may be the wrong metaphor to describe student behavior with regard to MOOCs. The fact that daily enrollments tripled the day edX president Anant Agarwal appeared on the popular TV comedy news program *The Colbert Report* indicates that many students are signing up for a MOOC out of curiosity, rather than a commitment to complete the course. And, as with other studies, the Harvard–MIT research confirms that students who demonstrate a desire to participate in class above and beyond auditing lecture videos (by taking the first assessment or completing the first writing assignment or problem set, for instance) pass at a much higher rate than the 5 to 10 percent of total enrollees who earn a certificate.

So if we consider people who engage in any activity beyond watching a video (such as turning in a homework exercise or taking a quiz) as demonstrating genuine interest in taking a MOOC course to completion, then attrition rates begin to look reasonable, especially when compared to behaviors associated with other free online activities. More important such calculations better reflect what students are actually doing in a course beyond just signing up for it.

While this might seem like good news for MOOC boosters, keep in mind that these statistics also demonstrate that the huge enrollment figures used by MOOC supporters to impress the press and public (not to mention investors) need to receive the same reality check used to calculate drop-out percentages. But we should also consider another academic reality that can be drawn from the numbers, one best summarized by Professor Pomerantz, whose UNC course analysis we just looked at:

> Before my MOOC launched, I did a quick back-of-the-envelope calculation of how many students I've ever had in the classroom, since I started teaching in grad school. And the number I came up with was, approximately 1,400. The number of students who completed my MOOC is approximately equal to the number of students I've had in the classroom *in my entire career*. The number of students who were *active* in the MOOC (Total Active Students) turned out to be approximately *an order of magnitude more* than the number of students I've had in the classroom in my entire career. Contemplate *that*.

Who Are MOOCs Educating?

Claims that MOOCs will utterly remake higher education imply that students who would have once applied to traditional (and expensive) colleges and universities will instead flock to free and flexible MOOCs. But as demographic information related to who is taking MOOC classes becomes available, it turns out that the traditional college level cohort of 18- to 22-year-olds represents just a small fraction of MOOC enrollees.

In a survey distributed at the end of MITx's popular Circuits and Electronics course (taught by edX president Agarwal), 7,161 students provided demographic information, including their age and level of education.[5] And while a little more than a quarter of students identified themselves as high-school graduates, 65 percent claimed BAs or advanced degrees as their highest level of education attained before taking the course. Now this survey was answered by less than 10 percent of total enrollees in the class, but close to 90 percent of those who filled out the survey also completed the course, indicating that descriptive statistics derived from the survey—including ages concentrated in the 20- to 40-year-old range—are good descriptors for those who signed up for the class intending to finish it.

In that aforementioned Edinburgh study, a personal information survey was also sent to 217,512 students who had enrolled in one or more of the six Coursera courses taught by the Scottish University. The survey generated 45,182 responses and also showed participation rates highest among people who were older and more educated than the demographics normally associated with college-age students (76% of respondents were over the age of 25 and 80% already had a BA or advanced degree).

Data available from the Harvard–MIT research studies mentioned earlier also demonstrate that at least 70 to 75

It turns out that the traditional college level cohort of 18- to 22-year-olds represents just a small fraction of MOOC enrollees.

percent of edX enrollees are beyond college age. But given the large total numbers of MOOC enrollees, the fact that 20 to 25 percent of students signing up for a massive course are high school or college age translates to a significant number of learners. However, many of these younger students participate in MOOCs as part of a classroom-based educational experience (such as a flipped classroom version of edX's Circuits taught at San Jose State University[6] or high-school and college programs in developing countries that use MOOC content for lecture material), which means the number of students looking at MOOCs as an independent-study alternative to traditional higher education may actually be smaller than overall statistics suggest.

These initial demographics seem to indicate that MOOCs are attracting an audience more likely to enroll in adult education or extension school programs or to participate in recreational learning, rather than the type of students who would be most affected if MOOCs provided a formal alternative to a traditional two- or four-year undergraduate program. The age and educational experience of so many MOOC students also invites questions regarding whether the training in how to learn one receives while enrolled in a higher educational program is required in order to succeed in a MOOC, a serious issue if MOOCs are going to be asked to serve as a substitute for that traditional college experience.

Additional data derived from these and other surveys indicate that variables such as gender can vary based on course topic (88% of those who identified gender in the edX Circuits survey were male compared to the nontechnology Edinburgh courses that were either evenly split by gender or skewed higher for women). And while participation by nation continues to be a topic of interest, county-by-country trends need to be looked at with an understanding that much of this international activity is institutional and driven by relationships that have been built by the MOOC providers or partner universities.

So while providing younger students access to inexpensive, high-quality education remains an important goal for MOOC creators and advocates, the natural audience for MOOCs seems to be an older and more educated cohort interested in advancing their learning, regardless of whether or not the work put into a MOOC leads to some type of officially recognized credential. But perhaps it is this lack of official recognition that is the cause of the trends just described—in which case, might these numbers change dramatically if students could obtain something with genuine "cash value" in the educational marketplace for completing a MOOC class, such as formally recognized college credit?

Credit for MOOCs

While the introduction of MOOCs and claims by some boosters of their equivalency to traditional college courses raised eyebrows and questions among educators, it was the attempt to turn those claims into the actual awarding of college credit that turned MOOCs from a curiosity to a subject of heated debate.

In March 2013, California state senator Darrell Steinberg introduced Senate Bill 520, which proposed creating a process that would be allow students in any of the state's institutions of higher learning (including California's University of California, California State University, and community college system) to use MOOCs as a substitute for classes that students could not get into because of overcrowding problems throughout the state college system.[7] Around that same time, legislators in Florida proposed a new system for accrediting online courses (including MOOCs) that could be used as substitutes for traditional classes at both the K–12 and college levels.[8]

Although these proposed bills were designed to help states deal with important local issues, the proposals triggered a national debate over whether free massive online courses from world-famous universities should be considered on a par with the residential and online programs offered by other (i.e., less prestigious) institutions of higher learning.

The association of MOOCs with organizations barely a year or two old (including for-profit companies such as Udacity and Coursera) made them an easy target, much like the way that for-profit textbook publishers often serve as a surrogate for attacks on the broader problem of increasing costs in higher education. But beyond economics and politics, the severity of the backlash against awarding MOOCs with college credit may have also derived from attempts to award them too much credibility too quickly.

After all, the advanced placement (AP) program, which dates to the 1950s, has been offering students a way to place out of intro-level college courses and even obtain actual college credit by passing expert-designed and graded rigorous exams. Mechanisms have long been in place allowing colleges to transfer credit, and programs that award college credit for independent study or life experience have been taking hold at many institutions, especially those trying to attract nontraditional learners such as veterans or returning older students.[9] And for many newer fields, especially in information technology, the ability to pass high-stakes certification exams has more cachet with employers than does where one went to school, just as professional licensure is more important in some fields than is a college degree.

There are also programs in place that allow organizations and institutions to accredit their courses for college-level equivalency, most notably the CREDIT program offered through American Council of Education (ACE).[10] The ACE accreditation process, which parallels state-level accreditation programs in terms of thoroughness and rigor, involves an analysis of course materials by a team of experts, often working on site for several days with teachers and course developers. And if a product is deemed creditworthy, the ACE team generates a recommendation of how many credit hours students should be awarded for completing the course, which is then published in a guide made available to member schools.[11] As this description implies, ACE awards *recommendations* rather than actual college credit, recommendations that the colleges and universities making up the membership of ACE are free to accept, reject, or modify (by rewarding more or fewer than the recommended number of credit hours).

In addition to ACE credit recommendations, credit-by-exam programs such as the College Board's College Level Examination Program (CLEP) or exam services from Excelsior College allow students to take exams in subjects ranging from introductory language and math to discipline-specific tests in subjects like nursing and philosophy. As with ACE credit recommendations, colleges and universities are free to decide whether they will count such awards toward a degree, and many limit the number of external credits one can apply to obtain a diploma.

What all of these programs have in common is that they require a student to be enrolled in an established college or university that has the choice of how much and what type of activity that takes place outside their institution will be allowed to count toward graduation requirements. And while schools are showing more flexibility as independent learning and academic exchange programs become increasingly popular, the effort required to turn success in one of these alternative learning experiences into credit at an institution is neither trivial nor free. Students who have completed an ACE accredited course, for example, need to pay ACE for a transcript that must then be presented to an institution that can choose whether to accept or reject that recommendation. Because many schools may not be familiar with the variety of credit-potential alternatives, students often have to sell their requests for credit to a skeptical administration or academic department. And even if they succeed, many colleges charge fees to apply alternative credentials toward a degree and limit the number of third-party credits that can count toward graduation. With so many hoops to jump through, only the most enterprising and entrepreneurial students—including those dedicated to cutting down time spent and thus the cost of college—tend to have the wherewithal to master both the course material learned through alternative study options and the bureaucratic procedures required to make that effort count toward a diploma.[12]

Even as states like Florida and California were considering ways to give MOOCs an accelerated on-ramp into the increasingly crowded field of credit equivalency, vendors such as Udacity and Coursera were doing the spadework necessary to gain recognition for some of their more popular courses, working with their academic partners to put several MOOCs through ACE accreditation[13] and forming partnerships with individual universities interested in giving students online alternatives for for-credit classes. But even in cases where a MOOC had been anointed with independent accreditation, the question remained as to whether or not any of those hundreds of thousands of MOOC enrollees had interest in turning their massive online learning experience into a formal college credit.

By the summer of 2013, the number of students requesting an ACE transcript containing a record of their completion of one or more MOOCs stood at zero. And when Udacity formed a partnership with Colorado State University–Global Campus to offer students the chance to earn credit by passing a Udacity computer programming course and paying a processing fee of $89 (versus the $1,000+ the school charged for an equivalent classroom course), again there were no takers.[14] It may be that any new academic program takes time to gain traction, but it is also possible that using alternative credits to trim just one (or even a handful) of courses from a two- or four-year-college lineup does not have enough of an impact on the total cost of an education to warrant taking the initiative to earn and apply MOOCs or other third-party programs to a degree.

As noted earlier, truly enterprising students can potentially use credit equivalency to earn a degree in less time, which translates to less cost. But students who demonstrate this level of entrepreneurial drive are increasingly choosing to skip college altogether, taking advantage of initiatives like the Thiel Fellowship, which offers students $100,000 grants for independent study projects that require they not go to college,[15] or the Uncollege program, started by Thiel Fellow Dale Stephens, which trains students for lifelong learning through self-study, mentoring, and entrepreneurship.[16]

While such radical anticollege initiatives might capture headlines (as well as the interest of students who, like Stephens, learned academic independence as part of the home-schooling movement), the bulk of college-bound high-schoolers still gravitate toward traditional degree programs, either residential or online. So even if MOOCs had managed to be immediately granted wholesale college equivalency through legislation proposed (and ultimately shelved or watered down) in places like California[17] and Florida,[18] they may just end up part of a matrix of college and college-credit alternatives within an evolving academic marketplace. And as parents and politicians continue to express anxiety over the inflationary spiral and accompanying debt associated with conventional higher education, MOOCs may play a role alongside other independent-learning alternatives with regard to more widespread educational reform.

For example, Michael Roth, president of Wesleyan University, has written about allowing students to graduate with a BA in three years versus four, or use four years at an institution to both obtain a BA and earn credit toward an advanced degree with independent study and other programs used to secure the credit needed to complete degree requirements.[19] While such a scheme would change the timeline traditionally associated with the college experience by creating cohorts of standard and accelerated learners within the same graduating class, such a change has the benefit of being revenue neutral for institutions. "I'm not sure exactly what the difference is between learning from a MOOC and learning from a 400 person lecture hall course at an expensive university,"[20] said Roth in an interview about his experience teaching a Coursera MOOC based on his popular Wesleyan course The Modern and the Postmodern. But if wider educational reform might create a MOOCs-for-credit market that currently does not exist, the question remains whether MOOCs have the academic rigor to be considered worthy enough to play a role in such a project.

Level of Demand

Before looking at how course rigor might be measured, it's important to keep in mind that questions regarding the full equivalency between a MOOC and a traditional college course are most relevant in the context of the MOOC-for-credit issues just discussed. Given that the vast majority of MOOC students are not interested in earning college credit, however, most MOOC participants look at level of demand in the context of determining whether or not a course can be completed within a required timeframe when class work must be juggled alongside other life responsibilities.

MOOCs of any length are always open to auditors (i.e., students interested solely in watching or listening to video lectures and who have no interest in earning a certificate of completion). But what separate MOOCs from various lecture-only alternative educational resources such as iTunes U are requirements beyond the lecture leading to some type of certificate. And when assessing MOOC rigor, keep in mind the observation made in chapter 3 that all MOOCs are not created to serve the same academic function. Some are built to mimic semester-long classes taught at established universities as much as possible, while others have the goal of teaching a subset of what might be included in a traditional semester-long class within a shorter (frequently 6- to 8-week) timeframe. Professors trying to replicate an existing residential course are more likely to try to fit into a MOOC as much syllabus content and as many assignments from the original course as the technology allows. In contrast, a professor interested in exposing a subject of passionate interest to large numbers of students might choose to limit workload in order to keep as many people in the class as possible.

This type of variability sets MOOCs apart from traditional college courses, where the semester system tends to impose standards regarding course length and credits, or credit hours are used to calibrate the amount of time and work associated with particular classes. Most of us attended colleges or universities featuring "gut" courses that were not particularly demanding and "grind" courses that asked far more from students than did more typical courses in a school's catalog. But as the negative connotation associated with both those terms implies, educational norms both within an institution and within the academy as a whole tend to create enough standardization to allow students to predict and balance the workload associated with the multiple courses they might be taking during a semester.

For MOOCs, course length tends to be an indicator of level of demand with courses running ten or more weeks (i.e., closer to the length of a full semester) often including more required reading, more frequent and difficult assessments, and more frequent use of creative assignments such as peer-graded essays or required contribution to online discussion boards. While even the shortest MOOC will ask students to fulfill obligations beyond watching video lectures, these are the courses where reading is more frequently optional and grading more likely to be based solely on passing a set of relatively easy weekly quizzes.

Engineering, science, and technology courses from MIT have traditionally been among the most demanding MOOCs. When Professors Eric Grimson and John Guttag offered their Introduction to Computer Science and Programming MOOC for edX, for example, they based the course on the same syllabus used in the residential version of that class. Lectures and assignments were largely identical between the two versions of the course, although adjustments needed to be made to allow programming assignments to be graded automatically. And many students who signed up for the course realized the 12 to 15 hours they were told to set aside each week for the class was a floor rather than a ceiling. In contrast, some of the social science and humanities courses I took for my Degree of Freedom One Year BA project ran for just 6 to 8 weeks, with each week's workload consisting of watching 1 to 2 hours of video lectures followed by a multiple-choice quiz, some of which contained fewer than ten questions.

As more MOOCs enter the marketplace, they seem to be spreading out across a continuum with regard to level of demand, with professors dramatically varying required versus optional reading, frequency and difficulty level of assessments, and the use of peer-graded essays and other creative assignments based on the goals of a course, the nature of the material, and professors' comfort level with options available to them through a chosen MOOC technology platform.

This wide variation in level of demand highlights the importance of independent accreditation through organizations like the American Council on Education when determining formal college course equivalence for a MOOC. And the majority of students who are not taking a MOOC for credit still need to be able to evaluate what will be asked of them when they choose to participate in a MOOC class if they want to avoid becoming one of those drop-out statistics discussed earlier in this chapter.

Regardless of their level of rigor, any course that is delivered remotely presents challenges regarding how to determine if a student is actually doing the required work. Confirming whether or not a student is reading assigned material is a challenge regardless of learning modality. But ensuring that students are not cheating on exams or plagiarizing on written assignments presents general challenges with all forms of online learning, and special problems when those online courses are being taken by tens of thousands.

Security—Cheating on MOOCs

In theory, one of the things that should make MOOCs less subject to cheating than traditional classroom or online courses is their lack of educational "cash value," at least during a period when obtaining recognized college credit for completing a MOOC is not a mainstream option.

The old adage that cheaters hurt only themselves is actually not true in an environment where something of value, such as credit toward a diploma, is at stake, since cheaters in those cases are actually helping themselves get to an end goal (graduation) while also hurting others by devaluing a grading system based on assumptions of integrity. But given that the vast majority of people who participate in a MOOC do so for their own edification, cheating in such an environment translates to behaving dishonestly in order to ensure one's own ignorance, all to obtain a certificate of completion that means very little to external audiences such as employers. It is all the more surprising, then, that cheating is perceived as rampant within MOOC courses.[21] But is that perception accurate? And even if cheating is infrequent, what could possibly motivate someone to cut corners in what is meant to be a self-directed personal learning experience with personal satisfaction the primary reward?

The sense that MOOCs invite cheating more than traditional classroom-based courses is built on public perception that assumes cheating is generally more widespread in online learning environments. But Bernard Bull, assistant vice president of academics and associate professor of educational design and technology at Concordia University, taught otherwise in a MOOC he created on the subject of cheating in online courses.[22] As I learned by taking that class, the professor's own research (based on survey data generated from the anonymous confessions of successful cheaters) indicates that self-reported cheating rates are no higher for online students than for students taking brick-and-mortar classes. This may be due to the fact that cheating rates are too high everywhere. Professor Donald McCabe's 2001 study of 4,500 high school and 1,800 college students found self-admitted cheating rates of 70 percent[23] and similar survey research found cheating to be even more prevalent among high-achieving students. And while other scholars have challenged sweeping claims based on numbers that might mix regretful once-in-a-lifetime plagiarists with serial cheaters, academic integrity seems to be a problem that transcends the role of technology in instruction.

Given that online learning technology has allowed students to take tests remotely, even in courses taken at residential colleges, the distinction between classroom-based and online education is becoming increasingly blurry (hence the popularity of the term "blended learning" to describe various hybrid teaching approaches that mix "live" and online course components). This means that graded tests that might have traditionally taken place inside a proctored classroom are frequently assigned as take-home exams that give students the opportunity to cheat unobserved, just as they have always been free to plagiarize in privacy. And speaking of plagiarism, this form of academic dishonesty not only makes up a huge percentage of cases of academic integrity code violations, it also represents a form of cheating that is most difficult to protect against.

Technology has generated an arms race between teachers trying to incorporate technology components into classroom instruction (or just give assignments in a world where the Internet is omnipresent) and students who can either use that technology to accelerate learning or to enable dishonest behavior such as buying completed assignments from so-called "paper mills" or simply cutting and pasting from third-party sources without attribution. But even as it enables various forms of dishonest behavior, technology also promises a solution in the form of plagiarism-detection software such as TurnItIn, which, when integrated into the teaching process, means professors get to review student work only after it has been given a clean bill of health from such third-party dishonesty-detection tools.

While anticheating products can save teachers the hours of work needed to sniff out plagiarized or purchased material in student assignments, such systems have the damaging effect of turning professors (who must confront students with the result of automated plagiarism evaluations) into policemen and students into suspects assumed to be guilty until TurnItIn declares them innocent. And the costs related to creating a culture of suspicion go beyond the risk of false accusations. For as Professor Bull related in class, his research indicates that the three major factors students take into account when deciding whether or not to cheat include laziness, risk, and student perception of lack of teacher engagement. While the first two factors are intuitive (students are tempted to cut corners if they can get the same grade by cheating rather than doing the actual work, and low chances of being caught correlate with higher likelihood of cheating), the third reason points out that when students feel a teacher is not respecting them (by just going through the motions in class or treating the student body as little more than grade-grubbing plagiarists), they are likely to return the favor by doing as little as possible to achieve a desired grade.

Some MOOCs get around these issues by taking advantage of the first of Bull's factors: laziness. If your entire grade on a massive online course is based on a set of short quizzes with an unlimited number of chances to get the right answers, or if exams provide immediate feedback regarding whether you answered a question incorrectly (and more chances to make the correct choice), scouring the Internet for posted answers to the test would actually involve more work than just guessing your way to a 100 percent score. And for test questions that might require additional help, forums are often full of hints that point students in the right direction (if not spelling out the answers outright).[24] While such activity could be described as collaborative, given that it facilitates some of the student-to-student teaching envisioned by the original MOOC pioneers, basing grades on assessments that can be easily gamed fits a time-tested teaching truism that says students are least likely to complain about a course being too easy.

As mentioned earlier, professors looking to increase the challenge level of a MOOC will often up their use of subjective assignments, such as peer-graded essays. But in addition to all of the issues mentioned in chapter 3 regarding peer evaluation (such as quality of scoring rubrics and variability of language skill among students), peer grading provides no method for detecting plagiarism beyond whatever effort the occasional experienced and/or paranoid peer grader might want to put into the task. This means that overt plagiarism, such as the copying and pasting of whole Wikipedia articles (something that would be caught immediately by a professor with or without a system like TurnItIn), might easily slip by students evaluating the work of other students.

Other than hoping self-motivation translates into academic integrity, MOOC providers are left relying on options like honor codes, which have shown limited utility in traditional classrooms, or technical Band-Aids such as Coursera's Signature Track program, which attempts to confirm that a student is submitting his or her own work, even if it cannot determine how many corners he or she may have cut to complete it.

Other emerging solutions to security issues have grown out of the response of professors throughout the academy to the plague of Internet-enabled plagiarism, solutions that involve creating new methods of evaluation that defy cutting and pasting. For instance, students who might have once been asked to turn in individual history assignments might work together to create an online version of a fictitious newspaper from the period being studied. Classroom presentations and digital video also offer ways for students to present what they have learned in public, providing a means for livening up a class through assignments that cannot be easily gamed. This is actually an area where MOOCs have considerable promise, for, as outlined in the following chapter, some professors involved with MOOC development have been looking at creative projects—some of which leverage the crowds of people taking the course—as a means to turn their online courses into unique and interesting assignments. In addition to limiting opportunities to cut corners, such creativity also helps demonstrate a professor's commitment to providing a meaningful learning experience with the hope that this will encourage honest work from an engaged student body.

Intellectual Property

As noted in the discussion of reading assignments in chapter 3, academic libraries frequently license databases of academic content for use within an institution. And reserve reading programs that allow libraries to lend out copyrighted material on a short-term basis are protected by legislation and regulation such as First-Sale Doctrine, the same doctrine that allows individuals to give away or sell legally purchased books or CDs to others without first seeking permission of copyright holders. But licensing arrangements and intellectual property rules put in place to allow schools flexibility with regard to sharing copyrighted material with enrolled students are not necessarily applicable to the student body of a MOOC, where most participants have no association with the institution that has created a course.

Another intellectual property issue related to MOOCs has to do with the third-party material professors might use in their lecture videos. Technically, any exhibit a professor includes in a classroom presentation, such as a photograph in a slide or music played in the classroom, is subject to copyright restrictions. Even before the advent of MOOCs, institutions have asked professors to secure rights for images, video and audio clips, and other materials used in a classroom, or make an effort to ensure the use of such content can be justified through legal principles such as fair use doctrine. This requirement has taken on additional urgency as MOOCs teaching tens of thousands up the level of risk for colleges and universities with regard to legal action related to intellectual property violations.

"Everything that is educational is not automatically fair use," says Kyle Courtney, copyright advisor to Harvard University, who has been advising HarvardX on the safe and legal use of copyrighted material within MOOC courses.[25] "It's the purpose and the character of your use, the nature of the content, the amount and substantiality of the portion taken, and the effect of the use on the market," he continues, describing the four factors used to ascertain coverage under a fair use doctrine—a doctrine often mistakenly believed to allow free reuse of content in any academic situation.

"We use the term 'window dressing' to describe something like a cartoon included in a slide show for a laugh which is aesthetic in principle, but not necessary to make your pedagogical point," continues Courtney, making a distinction between an exhibit like a photo used to highlight a point in literature and the use of that same picture to demonstrate an important principle relevant in a photography class. "When you're using a photo in a photography class, the photo takes on the point of the lesson."

Challenges arise, however, when the point of a lesson is subject to interpretation. For example, when Harvard's Greg Nagy, a professor of classics and an avid film buff, wanted to include scenes from *Blade Runner* in his edX MOOC The Ancient Greek Hero to illustrate a point about the timelessness of heroic mythology, an assessment of relevance that was clear to Nagy and his team needed confirmation through Harvard's copyright experts. This is why an assessment based on the four factors Courtney lists is a safer route than assuming educational relevance and hoping that a course broadcast to tens of thousands won't run afoul of a copyright holder's opinion on the matter.

Schools looking to use copyrighted works, either in video lectures or through syllabus reading, have a number of options they can pursue. "First, you can get permission from the copyright owner," says Courtney. "This usually takes time and might come with a number of restrictions. Publishers might ask 'What's a MOOC?' And most of these rights holders want to be paid for use of their material." Given that permission is not always attainable (or affordable for free MOOC classes), other alternatives include use of open access content or content owned by the institution developing the course, linking to external content, or asking those taking a course to obtain reading material on their own—an option that puts the burden of finding legal copies on the student rather than the university or MOOC provider.

Beyond questions of who owns material used within a MOOC are questions regarding who "owns" the MOOC itself, a product that includes content developed by a professor (who may be using selected third-party material) and produced by an institution for distribution through a third party such as edX or Coursera. While little is at stake financially when massive online courses are being given away to the public for free, as MOOC providers explore business models such as content licensing, questions are being asked regarding whether or not contracting arrangements between course providers and universities take into account ownership issues of all stakeholders, including those of the professors teaching the class. If a professor leaves a university, can he or she take the MOOCs they have created with them, or do recordings of his or her lectures remain the property of their former employer? Who is liable in the case of an intellectual property lawsuit: the professor, the school, or the MOOC provider? And if student-created content or data generated by or about a student builds value into a course or company, who owns the rights to these materials and data?

Perhaps some of these matters could be resolved if MOOCs fell into the category of truly open educational resources. But as with so much new terminology associated with MOOCs, the word "open" is open to interpretation.

Openness

While "open" may be one of MOOCs middle names, when this term is used in the context of massive open learning it usually describes a course with no barriers to participation with regard to costs, prerequisites, or any other requirements other than a desire to sign up.

When other technology-driven trends, such as open source software, open access journals, or open educational resources use the term "open," however, they are describing more formalized legal arrangements that support alternatives to market-based systems for distributing and using intellectual property. The open source movement, for example, was created to combat the increasing power of corporations producing and selling proprietary software. The Linux and Android operating systems, which are licensed to developers in ways that allow them to both use and modify source code, are examples of open source products that have become competitive with proprietary software from companies such as Microsoft and Apple. And in many industries, including education, open source solutions such as the Moodle learning management system have become major competitors to market-leading proprietary software products such as Blackboard.

If open source was created to break the monopoly of software giants, open access is a movement meant to offer an alternative to traditional publishers of academic journals who are perceived as having become too rapacious and restrictive in the absence of genuine competition.[26] Under open access rules, researchers can place their work in university-managed institutional repositories for free distribution, even as they also publish that same work in established journals. And a system of free open access journals that sometimes charge those submitting articles for services such as peer review and distribution rather than charging subscribers is gaining traction as an alternative to traditional academic and professional publishing business models.

Open educational resources (OER) is another system designed to allow educators to share materials based on flexible user licensing that allows resources to be used, modified, and distributed at no cost. MIT's OpenCourse-Ware initiative, which publishes syllabi, reading lists, homework assignments, tests, lecture notes, and (for some courses) video lectures, is probably the most well-known open education project, but repositories are growing that contain thousands of documents, data sources, problem sets, and other educational material for sharing, reuse, and repurposing. While some OER leaders see textbook publishers as playing the role monopoly software vendors and conventional journal publishers play for the open source and open access movements, it is not clear whether the open education branch of the open resource movement is meant to support or upend the traditional academy. This is why opinions regarding the genuine level of openness within MOOCs are mixed.

As was already pointed out, MOOC developers are already looking at open access content as a way to support putting required reading materials into the hands of students at no cost, demonstrating one intersection between MOOCs and the various open initiatives just described. And while some of the components of the software used to deploy MOOCs are proprietary, a trained eye can spot a number of free services (such as YouTube used to store and distribute many MOOC video lectures) that have been "mashed up" to create the MOOC experience. And in June 2013, edX announced that its complete learning management system would be made available under open source licensing, allowing third parties interested in building their own online learning libraries to leverage course-management tools and other resources already built into a system that has been proven out by Harvard and MIT. One of the first initiatives announced that would leverage the now-open edX LMS was MOOC.org, a partnership between edX and Google that is promising to allow anyone to create a course that can be deployed through edX software running on Google servers. Such a service would compete with companies such as Udemy that also allow anyone to create and deploy a course, although it remains to be seen if the free MOOC.org service will attract developers of academic courses rather than the type of commercial training developers that make up the bulk of Udemy content providers.

Despite their overlaps with various open movements, MOOCs themselves are not made available under OER licensing arrangements that would allow third parties to modify and deploy them without restriction. While MOOC providers are encouraging use of their content in formal learning environments through initiatives like Coursera's Learning Hub program, they are also negotiating paid licensing arrangements with colleges and universities interested in utilizing MOOC content in whole or in part.

Of all the controversies noted in this chapter, arguments regarding MOOC levels of openness mostly take place within more rarified educational circles. But even those most eager to see open education disrupt an educational economy characterized by out-of-control costs and runaway educational debt must start their mission by first asking what it is that colleges and universities actually sell.

What Are Colleges Selling?

Someone making the case that the primary value of a college experience derives from the classes offered there could calculate the value of each course by simply dividing annual tuition and fees by (on average) the eight full-semester courses a student takes each year, which works out to approximately $2,000 per course at a state institution and up to $5,000 per course at an Ivy League college. As noted earlier in this chapter, however, students and parents do not seem to be doing this math since, if they did, MOOCs-for-credit programs and similar low-cost independent learning alternatives that would allow students to "buy" credits for pennies on the dollar would likely be met by something other than indifference. So if colleges and universities are worth their high price tags, what are they actually selling beyond classroom versions of courses increasingly being given away for free?

One of the most intriguing aspects of the MOOC phenomenon is that it has required colleges and universities to better understand and articulate the nature of their "product," especially for schools selling the value of their own residential learning experiences while also making claims about the rigor and value of MOOCs being given away at no cost. Sanjay Sarma, director of digital learning at MIT (a role that gives him responsibility over programs such as MITx and MIT's OpenCourseWare initiative) has been at the forefront of making the case that "there is essential magic in residential in-person education that is difficult to articulate, let alone replicate online." This "Magic Beyond the MOOCs"[27] includes the kinds of hands-on, collaborative experiences required in all disciplines, collaboration that in the case of Sarma's own institution has led to founding of many companies by MIT students bringing work they created together in school labs to market after graduation. Given his responsibility to both expand the reach of the university through initiatives like MITx and simultaneously find ways this same technology can be used to enhance residential learning, Sarma highlights that a "key benefit of online instruction is increased time for face-to-face interaction, making it possible to further enrich the residential experience." As an example of this phenomenon, he points out that edX has become the most popular educational application within MIT used to flip courses by moving the lecture component of a course outside of class, giving students more time to work with professors and one another in those places where experiential learning puts the information delivered via lecture into practice.

Those making the case against MOOCs face the same challenge as Sarma: explaining the value of the traditional college experience, an experience that has become increasingly costly even as one of the key components of that experience (the course) has become the latest media-based content to be commoditized via the Internet. And the list of things that allegedly make a college experience uniquely valuable, including the friends and contacts made during college years, the opportunity for intellectual exploration, the chance to wrestle with ideas and challenges through interaction with fellow students under the guidance of learned professors, must justify not just the residential college experience itself but the ever-growing price tag associated with partaking in that experience.

What most of the academics, administrators, and educational policy makers articulating these cases have in common is first-hand experience with the residential programs they champion, given that most participated in four-year residential degree programs between the ages of 18 and 22. But with the growth and diversification of higher education over the last several decades, which has led more and more students—including older students—to choose two- as well as four-year programs at commuter schools or online universities, almost half of those enrolled in college

One of the most intriguing aspects of the MOOC phenomenon is that it has required colleges and universities to better understand and articulate the nature of their "product."

today fall outside the archetypical college career that is being contrasted with the "impersonal" nature of MOOCs.

Then there is the paradox at the heart of higher education best articulated by Anya Kamenetz in her 2010 book *Diy U: Edupunks, Edupreneurs, and the Coming Transformation of Higher Education*,[28] a pre-MOOC manifesto for a do-it-yourself "edupunk" movement that encourages competition with a higher education system that she claims is pricing itself out of reach while failing to deliver what it promises.

> The nation's top colleges seem to assent to the signaling hypothesis when they agree to rate themselves by how selective they are—that is, how many people they reject, the SAT scores of entering students, and so on. That's like Weight Watchers advertising that they only take skinny people. If elite schools really subscribed to the value-added, human-capital theory, wouldn't they instead advertise how good they are at improving the very low SAT scores of entering students? Wouldn't they say: "We can take absolutely anyone and use our proven teaching materials to turn them into Swarthmore or Pomona material?"

This higher education paradox points out a contradiction at the heart of a college (prestige or otherwise) claiming to offer a unique and valuable service with regard to the quality education they deliver. For if the staff and teaching techniques offered at Harvard or Princeton are indeed so remarkable as to demand hundreds of thousands of dollars in the marketplace, then why shouldn't those people and techniques work for anyone partaking in such pedagogically powerful programs?

But most prestige colleges and universities *do not* offer their allegedly effective products to any and all. Rather, they limit their customer base to only those who have already proven themselves academically, which means their "customers" would likely succeed in any learning environment. This brings up the question of whether big-name educational institutions with highly discriminating admissions processes are actually "selling" education or discrimination.

One of the strongest cases that can be made in support of MOOCs is that they solve this paradox by allowing anyone access to high-quality courses previously available only to those able to get past the gate keepers barring entry to prestigious (and expensive) colleges and universities. In fact, MOOCs provide students the flexibility to choose classes from multiple institutions, rather than being restricted to just the set of courses offered by the residential college they were lucky enough to be accepted into. And even if courses alone do not make up the totality of a college experience, they certainly have more educational value for the thousands of people who have completed them than their zero-dollar price tags would imply.

A CULTURE OF EXPERIMENTATION

As the quotes that ended chapter 3 indicate, those involved with the MOOC project have always highlighted the importance of research and experimentation when explaining the value of massive online learning to educational constituencies as well as to the public. This chapter takes a closer look at what some of this investigation, trial, and error looks like to determine whether a culture of experimentation can be considered the differentiator between MOOCs and other forms of online learning.

As centralized programs with hundreds of thousands of participants, MOOCs are generating the type and volume of data needed to perform meaningful statistical analysis regarding what students are doing in their online classes. At the same time, surveys and other forms of research involving large numbers of students participating in such classes can answer questions that begin with "who," "how," and "why."

In addition to collecting and analyzing data, developers of MOOC classes have also demonstrated a desire to quickly put those research results to work, modifying course components based on how effective they were in previous iterations of a class, or tinkering with class structure and assignments to take into account best practices developed in other courses. This culture of experimentation has also created an environment where course developers are eager to test out new teaching ideas and share their results (either data driven or experiential), allowing MOOC designers to try new things that appear to work well while also learning from other people's mistakes. And as anyone who has seen typos, programming errors, or on-the-fly changes to their massive courses already knows, those who sign up for a free MOOC get to play the dual role of student and beta tester.

Research

You have already read about some of the statistical research that has come out of the earliest MOOC courses. For example, the University of Edinburgh study described in chapter 4, which shed light on the demographics surrounding the student body of a MOOC course, was based on data generated by Coursera's learning management system supplemented by the results of surveys received from tens of thousands of class participants. Researchers at Coursera (including the company's cofounders) also published a study in June 2013 entitled "Retention and Intention in Massive Open Online Courses: In Depth," which used data-driven "heat maps" to analyze some of the retention and student behavior issues discussed in detail in the previous chapter.[1]

The first-year research findings from HarvardX and MITx, also mentioned in the previous chapter, provide the most detailed analysis of who is participating in MOOC classes and what they do after enrolling.[2] As Justin Reich, an MIT lecturer and HarvardX research fellow, explains, these results

> extend findings from previous research teams, in striking ways. The percentage of students who finish a course through HarvardX is pretty similar to MITx, to U Penn's and University of Edinburgh's Coursera results. The proportion of people who already have an advanced degree, the tilt toward men, the fact that our students are older than a typical college student, all of that seems to be pretty consistent with what other folks have found.
>
> I hope the special contribution of our research is to characterize all of the different ways that people are using MOOCs as learners, with some pathways that lead to certification and other pathways that

lead to meaningful learning without certification. If we're going to understand how open online learning experiences are contributing to society then we can't just narrowly focus on certification. We have to try to figure out all the different ways people are learning and having a meaningful experience.[3]

While one of the research papers published by Harvard/MIT presents aggregate results across multiple courses, others present reports for each individual MOOC class. These detailed papers about particular courses highlight what Reich refers to as "a diversity of teacher and course intention," reflecting the fact that just as students spread out across a spectrum of activity (from dabblers to auditors to students who complete far more work than is necessary to achieve a passing grade), MOOCs themselves spread out across a continuum of intention: some professors are trying to reproduce their residential experience online while others are trying to create learning experiences that don't have the same structures or goals as their residential counterparts. As Reich points out, "The results from individual massive courses should be viewed as reflecting the diverse goals of the professors and teaching teams behind each course."

In addition to these descriptive studies, researchers are also looking at new ways of defining educational behavior based on the unique environments of large-scale classes. For example, a working paper entitled "Changing 'Course': Reconceptualizing Educational Variables for Massive Open Online Courses,"[4] written by members of MIT's Teaching and Learning Laboratory and Harvard's Graduate School of Education, used information from the first generation of MOOCs as the basis for proposing how terms such as "enrollment" and "curriculum" need to be redefined in the context of open massive online learning. And another MIT study, entitled "MOOCdb: Developing Data Standards for MOOC Data Science,"[5] used existing MOOC data as the basis for proposing a set of standards that could support ongoing research in different areas of MOOC-based education.

As MOOCs gained momentum throughout 2012 and 2013, researchers working independently of the MOOC providers or the colleges and universities participating in MOOC development have been organizing their own channels for publishing and funding research. For instance, in September 2013 the new academic journal *MOOCs Forum* released its premiere issue with articles on subjects like adaptive learning and alternative means of assessment within MOOCs.[6] And as that journal was being announced, a new Bill and Melinda Gates Foundation–funded MOOCs research initiative (MRI) was awarding its first set of $10,000 to $25,000 grants to over two dozen independent researchers working on issues related to assessment, engagement, retention, and personalized learning, as well as the role MOOCs can play with communities outside their traditional college niche such as K–12 educators and employers.[7]

Some of this research has focused on a single attribute of a MOOC class. Discussion comments, for example, were the basis of the Piazza study described in chapter 3, an MIT Teaching and Learning Lab project designed to classify MOOC discussion posts for easier analysis,[8] and an article in the premiere issue of *MOOCs Forum* entitled "Crowd-sourcing to Assess MOOCs: A Position Paper"[9] that looked at how forum activity could be used as a basis for grading class participation. And Gates-funded MOOC research initiative grants have gone toward projects that look at course components such as peer grading, community formation, and assessment, in addition to ongoing analysis of key issues such as student motivation and retention.

Not all research into MOOCs has delivered what MOOC supporters would categorize as good news. Most notably, a National Science Foundation (NSF)–funded research study that evaluated the use of three Udacity's courses (two in math, one in statistics) as the basis of a MOOCs-for-credit program at San Jose State University (SJSU) demonstrated failure rates much higher in MOOC-based courses than in conventional classes on the same subjects.[10]

Unsurprisingly, the harshest MOOC critics simply added the SJSU results to their bill of indictment. But lost in all the heated discussion over the NSF study was the fact that students participating in the program included both matriculated students at SJSU (whose pass rates ranged from 29.8 percentto 54.3 percent, depending on the course) and younger students from a partner high school serving economically disadvantaged youth (whose pass rates ranged from 11.9 percent to 48.7 percent). Just as important, the purpose of that that experiment was not to create a John Henry–style match-up between online and live-classroom teachers, but "to assess the effectiveness of human mentorship and guided peer interaction in the context of Massive Open Online Courses (MOOCs)." In other words, those engaged with this project understood that "(a) MOOCs are [currently] more successful for highly self-motivated individuals; [and] (b) there is a nearly complete absence of interactive human mentoring in MOOCs," which is why their research project was designed to test the effectiveness of options like 1:1 mentoring or guided discussion via video conferencing as *supplements* to MOOC training.

The results of this experiment, coupled with the general anti-MOOC backlash underway when the results were released, contributed to a cooling of enthusiasm for MOOCs-for-credit programs in places like California. But even as that story was playing out, a less high-profile experiment in which another San Jose State professor used content from MITx's Circuits and Electronics course as a component of a flipped classroom was showing very positive results, leading to an expansion of the program within the University of California system.[11] And the same Udacity content used to anchor the original NSF project is also being made available to professors interested in using it as part of blended-learning versions of traditional classroom courses.[12] So even as some aspects of this research served to humble those proposing MOOCs as an alternative to residential degree programs, other results indicate that online content being generated by some of the world's best colleges and universities might do the most good by playing a supporting, rather than a starring, role in existing classroom-based and blended courses.

Experimentation

Unlike a great deal of academic research that gets circulated only to small communities that might not focus on it for months or years (if ever), research related to MOOCs can find its way into products almost immediately.

Sergiy Nesterko, a research fellow at HarvardX, is a statistician who has been looking at what data derived from hundreds of thousands of students taking dozens of courses might tell us about student behavior in the MOOC environment. "Research is one of the three cornerstones of

HarvardX," explains Nesterko, alluding to founding principles that also include teaching and learning.[13]

> And the research we have done has had a direct impact on course development. For example, our research team took a look at ten courses, five from Harvard and five from MIT, courses which took different approaches to how assignments were scheduled. Some of them put hard deadlines on every assignment, while others left all assignments open for the entire length of the course. And the data seemed to show that courses with fixed deadlines had higher completion rates. Now this is a correlation, so we would have to do some experimentation to prove causality. But once we shared our findings with the HarvardX course teams, they were eager to talk to us about their philosophies behind scheduling assignments and start looking at how to build what we learned into future courses. They were also very open to discussing how we might be able to create structured experiments in order to discover if there actually is a causal relationship between deadlines and success in a course.

Just as data-driven research and development is one source for innovation within the MOOC community, the developers of massive online classes are also tapping their own creativity to come up with experiments that leverage resources and large numbers of participants associated with MOOCs to create novel, innovative learning experiences. In chapter 3, we looked at how experiments with instructional formats are taking place in the area of video-based lecturing where shorter lectures or videos based on dialogs, interviews, on-location shots, and even skits and performances are blending with or replacing traditional sage-on-stage presentations. But lectures are not the only area where professors are trying to create a MOOC experience that cannot be replicated in a traditional college classroom.

For instance, when professors Walter Sinnott-Armstrong of Duke University and Ram Neta of University of North Carolina at Chapel Hill first gave their popular Coursera class Think Again: How to Reason and Argue, they came up with a novel idea for a creative class project to accompany the automatically scored quizzes and homework assignments that contributed to student grades. Rather than ask students to submit examples of arguments for one-to-one peer grading, they instead announced an argument contest that would allow students to submit written or video-recorded arguments into a special folder set up in the course's discussion forum. The arguments had to demonstrate one or more principles of critical thinking taught in the class and the student body was enlisted to vote submissions up and down with the top-performing arguments dissected by the professors in the last week of the class as a final demonstration of all the techniques and tools taught over the previous eleven weeks. While participating in this contest was voluntary (and thus ungraded), the 500+ arguments submitted by students, which ranged from the philosophical ("Humans are innately good") to the theological ("God—logically proven") to the whimsical ("Vegetarians should not drive") represented one of the first successful uses of crowdsourcing (defined as a centrally directed effort leveraging large groups of people) within a MOOC class.[14]

Professor Cathy Davidson, also from Duke University, is the author of *Now You See It: How Technology and Brain Science Will Transform Schools and Business for the 21st Century* and a leading advocate for technology-based educational transformation.[15] In her 2014 MOOC class, entitled The History and Future of (Mostly) Higher Education, she also planned to leverage a student body of tens of thousands to implement a crowdsourced project only possible in a massive learning environment. "I'm actually trying to turn the camera around so that the students, and we think there will be fifty or a hundred thousand of them, are part of the process of making the future of higher education. So the assignments include things like a timeline that goes back to 1800 where one assignment will be to find something really interesting that happened in your country or county or state or locality in a ten year period and put it on our timeline," said Davidson in a 2013 interview that took place while her course was in development.[16] "To my knowledge, there has never been a timeline with 50,000 people contributing information about events in their local education arrayed in this way. I think it's going to be an incredibly interesting—if anecdotal—research tool for the future. So I like being able to use the MOOC in that way: using massive in a helpful way, not just one person talking to the masses but massive numbers of people contributing to a new kind of history."

Professors are also experimenting with ways to include components in their classes that defy common wisdom regarding what can and cannot be taught in any online course, much less a massive course in which students do not have direct contact with the teacher. Professor David Cox of Harvard, who has included on-location shooting and interactive exercises in the video components of his 2013 HarvardX MOOC Fundamentals of Neuroscience, also wanted to give students the ability to engage in real-world experimentation as part of the class. "In addition to asking students to interact with rich simulations, we are also asking students to do experiments in real life. Now many courses, including online courses, have textbooks and those cost up to $100. We're basically telling people don't buy a textbook," explained Cox in a 2013 interview.[17]

If you're going to spend any money on this course, what you should buy is this lab kit that [comes from a company] we partnered with called Backyard Brains and what this kit lets you do, fairly inexpensively, is to run real-life neuroscience experiments at home using invertebrates (cockroaches, worms, things like that). What we're doing is to invite students to do the experiments, we're providing lab manuals and video demonstrations, and then we're having students do these experiments at home and then we're encouraging them to film their experiments and send them to us.

As with courses that involve copyrighted textbooks, activities that might cost money (such as readings that are not in the public domain or use of a $100 experimental lab kit) are optional within Harvard's Neuroscience MOOC. But in addition to innovating within his class, Professor Cox also experimented with a new means of fundraising on behalf of students taking his course. "Not everyone in the world can afford these [lab kits], and it's certainly not a required component of the course. But we wanted to have as many people from as many kinds of backgrounds doing this. So, to that end, we started a Kickstarter campaign," continues Cox, describing his use of a third-party crowd-funding site, "to raise money to buy these kits for as many people as we can around the world." The campaign was a success, raising over $14,000, which meant that free kits were made available to over a hundred students, on top of the many students who purchased kits on their own.

In theory, this use of paid material creates a distinction between students who can afford to take full advantage of everything the MOOC has to offer and those who cannot. But given that Cox's campaign represents one of the few instances of a MOOC earning rather than just costing money, his experience also points to another question MOOC developers are trying to answer through experimentation: how to get these free learning tools to break even or even turn a profit.

Business Model Experiments

A new online venture attracting millions of signups—seemingly overnight—tends to generate expectations that turning mass audiences into mass revenue is just a matter of developing an effective, scalable business model and finding the right investors and management team to implement it.

Much of the business-focused discussions surrounding MOOCs have centered on the ways major MOOC providers such as Udacity, Coursera, and edX can turn their popularity into the dollars needed to sustain a multimillion-dollar enterprise and, in the case of venture-funded companies like Udacity and Coursera, turn a profit. But there are other economic players with a stake in the success or failure of MOOCs, notably the colleges and universities who create (and usually own) the courses distributed by those providers, educational institutions whose goals and financial requirements might be different from those of a Coursera or an edX. And the MOOC field is becoming an increasingly crowded space, with new providers such as the UK's FutureLearn and Germany's iversity releasing European MOOC content alongside US ventures such as Canvas and Udemy, which straddle the line between paid and free open learning. And as LMS providers such as Blackboard and Moodle explore how to open up courses on their system to the world, new players such as the edX-Google partnership MOOC.org are promising to provide a way for anyone to become a MOOC professor—an exciting opportunity for educators but a confounding factor for business people trying to attach a price tag to courses that are becoming increasingly commoditized. Finally, increasing numbers of Internet startups, major corporations (including educational publishers), and entrepreneurial nonprofits are looking at the student body of MOOCs as potential clients for their products and services.

The business models that have been subject to the most experimentation involve the major MOOC providers trying to create products they can sell to students or ways of packaging their content to sell to institutions. For-credit programs, like those offered through the University of Phoenix, demonstrate a market for fee-based degrees offered entirely online. But the ability to sell, rather than just give away, noncredit academic courses also has precedent represented by the success of organizations like the Teaching Company, which has been selling its Great Courses college-level lectures since the 1990s (and continues to sell them, even as phenomena like iTunes U and MOOCs create free alternatives). But there is also precedent for failure, notably the experience of AllLearn, a partnership between Yale and Oxford Universities that shut its doors in 2006 after failing to convince learners that courses that might cost thousands if taken at either institution were worth just a few hundred dollars to take online.[18]

AllLearn was doing math similar to what you saw at the end of the last chapter, where the value of a course was derived by dividing the cost of a year at college by the number of courses one would take while being enrolled at an Oxford or Yale. But as that analysis pointed out, the "special something" frequently invoked as being part of the on-campus college experience clearly has cash value in the marketplace where students (and parents) willing to pay $25,000 to $50,000 a year to attend a school balk at paying less than a hundred dollars for a MOOC associated with actual college credit. So if no one seems ready to spend thousands, or even hundreds, to take a MOOC, might someone be willing to pay anything to take one? And if so, how much?

If you consider the partnerships between Udacity and San Jose State University and the University of Colorado described in the previous chapter as business-model experiments, they seem to indicate that even when colleges were ready to accept MOOCs for credit, student demand was minimal. But if college-age students represent, at best, a developing future market, what about the 70 to 80 percent of MOOC enrollees who are older and already have a degree? Is there anything MOOC-related that they might hand over their credit card in order to obtain?

HarvardX offers options for students to earn a special certificate (for $350) or an actual credit through the Harvard Extension School (for $2,050) if they pass the popular CS50x Introduction to Computer Science course, leveraging the institution's ability to provide extension school credit that still bears a Harvard imprimatur. And MIT announced a new Online X program (which leverages both the MIT and "X" brands) offering technology and business courses designed for professionals.[19] The first Online X offering, called Tackling the Challenges of Big Data (and priced at $495), was scheduled to begin in March of 2014 and, as with Harvard's experiments with CS50x, it remains an open question whether people will pay for a course when comparable MOOC content is available for free.

Even as those new products were being introduced, the experimental "student-pays" business model tapping an older demographic most successfully was Coursera's Signature Track program. As mentioned previously, Signature Track does not provide students with college credit but instead adds a stamp of approval to the certificate a student earns when completing certain Coursera MOOCs, one that affirms that a Signature Track student was actually the person who performed the work required in the class. The security measures used to earn this stamp include asking students to provide digital images to confirm they are the ones submitting assignments, as well as a system for comparing a student's typed submissions with a keyboarding "fingerprint" that is supposed to be unique to every typist. While Signature Track has huge holes as a security system compared to even simple classroom proctoring, the program has succeeded in building value—$30–$100 to be exact—by adding some level of validation into an otherwise-free MOOC certificate of completion. And, at the start of 2014, Coursera introduced a specialization program covering areas like data science, cybersecurity, and foundations of teaching and learning that allows students who earn Signature Track certificates for a specified set of courses to earn an additional credential by completing all course work as well as a "capstone project" associated with each specialization program.[20]

Even before the introduction of specializations (which creates an intriguing new credential representing more than a course, but less than a degree), Signature Track generated $1 million in revenue for Coursera by the end of 2013. And while this represented less than 5 percent of the venture capital the company obtained that same year, the Signature Track experiment established the existence of a segment of the MOOC student body ready to pay for recognition regarding their completion of a massive online course.

Information regarding what motivated over 25,000 students to purchase Signature Track validated certificates in 2013 is anecdotal, but evidence seems to suggest that those seeking this higher level of certification plan to use the document in some kind of professional capacity.[21] Such behaviors provide evidence for the notion that even people willing to spend hundreds of hours on self-improvement through independent study are ready to spend money only on things that will help them advance professionally. Other evidence for this phenomenon includes the financial success of paid online training vendors such as Lynda.com, whose learning library focuses on technical and design skills that provide a low-cost alternative to classroom training for employees or job seekers. And if you look over the thousands of courses offered by Udemy, a site that allows anyone to post a course and charge whatever he or she likes for it—including nothing—you will find a few thousand people signing up to take a free academic course on subjects like ancient Greek religion or the works of T. S. Eliot, compared to the 50,000 to 100,000 people ready to pay $99 each to learn how to use Microsoft Excel.

If MOOCs ever gain traction with credit options that allow them to sit alongside other money-earning programs such as CLEP or AP, this could open up more business-to-consumer (or, in modern business parlance, B2C) opportunities for MOOC providers beyond the professional development opportunities that seems to be driving programs like Signature Track. In the meantime, might some business-to-business (B2B) sales models generate revenue by selling to someone other than students?

One model explored by all the major MOOC providers involves licensing content to schools. For example, Coursera struck licensing deals with California's Antioch College as well as several state college systems that allow those institutions to include MOOCs in their catalogs with licensing fees shared between Coursera and the schools and professors that created the licensed material.[22] Similarly, edX has explored a number of licensing models that would allow schools to leverage edX content in their own flipped classrooms experiments.[23] Licensing content to international universities has also been explored by MOOC providers, even as they continue to offer this same material for free to school systems in countries with limited educational resources. But licensing deals that assumed revenue would be generated by students paying to obtain college credit for MOOC classes have run into the problems noted earlier of limited interest in fee-based MOOCs-for-credit programs. And it was the licensing arrangement between edX and the California higher education system that triggered the revolt of the San Jose State philosophy department that marked the beginning of the MOOC backlash described in chapter 1.

Content licensing based on teacher reuse of MOOC lectures and other resources may also be limited by how quickly and widely teachers embrace the flipped classroom model, which assigns watching video lectures as homework, freeing class time for extended discussion or work on in-class projects. Even in cases where teachers are eager to move lecturing out of the classroom, professors are frequently creating their own lecture videos or turning to resources from the open web (which includes many of the same lectures found within MOOC classes) to broaden the number of voices students hear during a course. In fact, some professors are using content they generate to create their own MOOC-like classes, meaning the flipped classroom may present competition as well as opportunity to the major MOOC organizations.[24]

Traditional "passive income" opportunities such as online advertising or the sale of e-mail lists are unlikely business models for educational programs whose credibility rests on a perceived mission of altruism, although an affiliate marketing program that earns a percentage from textbook sales channeled through the online retailer Amazon generates $70,000 annually for MIT's open courseware program. And Udacity has allowed students to opt into a career placement program that allows the company to share data with headhunters seeking skilled job candidates, with the other MOOC vendors also exploring similar employment-related business models. Unlike various "pennies-per-click" income schemes, candidate sourcing and placement is high dollar per transaction. But it remains to be seen if employer interest in MOOC students extends beyond a few hot areas like computer programming. It is also unclear if companies founded to create and deliver educational content are ready to become players in a crowded, complex, and competitive employment industry.

Before we leave the topic of business experimentation, you should keep in mind that the people participating in such experiments extend beyond the most well-known MOOC companies. For instance, the MOOC phenomenon triggered the creation of a number of Internet startups offering products such as educational portfolios or services such as tutoring to help fill holes in the MOOC ecosystem. Several of these companies are based on the same generate-traffic-now/figure-out-how-to-monetize-later strategy that MOOC providers have chosen, which means they are struggling with similar issues of how to make money off a population that has so far demonstrated only its willingness to get something for nothing. And, as mentioned during discussions of reading and intellectual property, major educational publishers are experimenting with their own MOOC business models with companies like Viking Penguin offering a free electronic version of Cathy Davidson's book to the first 50,000 students who enroll in her Future of Higher Education Coursera MOOC, a business model experiment based on the hope that a significant percentage of MOOC students will opt to buy her book from the publisher when the course finishes. In October of 2013, the scientific, technical, and medical publishing giant Elsevier agreed to provide open access to published book content for up to five edX courses.[25] And the MIT Press, after taking over publishing for a textbook written by John Guttag for his edX course Introduction to Computer Science and Programming Using Python, offered an electronic version of the full text for free to students enrolled in the class and later went on to sell 10,000 hard-copy and electronic editions of the book to students enrolled in the author's MOOC.

Finally, colleges and universities taking part in free-learning projects are not looking toward royalty checks alone as their only potential source of income. David Cox's Neuroscience course, for example, demonstrated that there is no harm in simply asking people participating in a MOOC to spend their own money to get something of value. Examples of other school-initiated revenue efforts include a request for donations sent by Wesleyan University president Michael Roth to students who participated in his Coursera MOOC The Modern and the Postmodern and e-mail campaigns and a donation button that are part the fundraising program for MIT's OpenCourseWare initiative. And the glitzy video Harvard produced to showcase its HarvardX efforts during its latest $6.5 billion development drive demonstrates that institutions involved with MOOCs can always fall back on their most reliable mode for generating cash: asking people of means to write a check.

Pedagogical Experiments

Most of the experiments described in this chapter represent attempts to try new pedagogies for a new instructional medium. Online learning had already created physical distance between teachers and students, but it still allowed for one-to-one or small-group interaction through the creative use of online communication tools. But with MOOCs, the size of classes required new approaches to teaching that assumed direct interaction between an instructor and his or her students would not be part of the teaching dynamic.

Attempts to innovate instructional videos so that they do something other than deliver the same content as a podium lecture or experiments involving a large student body participating in crowdsource-style projects represent some of the pedagogical innovations that have made MOOCs unique learning experiences. And while some experiments have confirmed that massive online instruction is not likely to be effective for all types of learners, the continued popularity of MOOCs indicates that distance instruction featuring hugely enrolled classes can be effective for certain populations of students.

Within the world of massive online courses, the techno-geeky term of SPOC (small private online course) was coined to describe the implementation of MOOC content in something other than a 100 percent open-enrollment environment. For instance, a HarvardX SPOC on intellectual property law, called CopyrightX, limited enrollment to just 500 students who had to apply to take the course and participate in weekly discussions and pass a final exam (graded by the teaching team) in order to earn a certificate. This somewhat loose term has also been used to describe the use of MOOC content as a component of classroom courses like the aforementioned Circuits course taught in San Jose State University, as well as other instances where MOOCs materials are used as part of a flipped-classroom implementation.

The flipped classroom is a pedagogical experiment that has been mentioned a number of times in this book. If you recall, flipping the class refers to a method of instruction that reverses the typical order in which students listen to lectures while in class and then work on homework elsewhere with a new model that has them watch lectures on video in their homes or dorms, freeing class time for discussion and projects that involve more interactivity between teachers and students.

Flipping got a major boost in 2011 when the concept was embraced by Salman Khan, who proposed it as a strategy for making effective use of the short video lectures in his growing Khan Academy library, videos that have been finding a home at various points in the learning process.[26] And if the notion of using class time to do something other than listen to a teacher talk sounds familiar, that is because most of the classes all of us took from kindergarten through much of high school involved using class time to do more than sit while a sage teacher instructed us from behind a lectern. But as those high school years ended and college began, those teachers were replaced by professors, many of whom spent much of their adult lives training to deliver specialized knowledge to eager classrooms full of students. This dynamic might explain why some of the professors who love lecturing the most are the very ones attracted to teaching massive open courses that give them an even bigger audience to speak before. But it also highlights a challenge for those proposing the new flipped model, namely, how to get professors who love (and are used to) having their live talking as the focal point of the class to instead dedicate class time to doing something else.

This transition is probably easiest for professors flipping their own class since this simply involves moving their personal voice from one part of a course to another. But even here, most MOOC professors have yet to flip their own classrooms even after creating content that they claim can facilitate the flipping of someone else's. There are exceptions. For example, Peter Bol, who serves as Harvard's vice provost of advanced learning (which gives him responsibility over HarvardX), has integrated the material he created for his edX course on the history of China into a now-flipped classroom-based version of that same course. And as flipping allowed for more in-class discussion, Professor Bol began including video recordings of some of those discussions in the MOOC itself, demonstrating some of the intriguing two-way communication options opened up by the flipped-classroom model.

At the same time, when MOOC content is presented as a tool for flipping other people's classes, professors (like those in the philosophy department at San Jose State) are legitimately wondering what their role is supposed to be if Michael Sandel or some other Ivy League "rock star professor" is given the job of delivering the bulk of course content via videos the flipped professors had no involvement in creating.

One group frequently described as being threatened by MOOCs are community college professors who fear that once a classroom has been flipped they will end up at the bottom as little more than glorified paper graders. But such an argument ignores the fact that teachers at such institutions are often far more innovative and entrepreneurial than their Ivy League colleagues. Online learning took hold fastest within this segment of higher education, and even before the advent of MOOCs many teachers at community or small state colleges were eagerly experimenting with how to integrate third-party content into their classes. In fact, whole disciplines (such as the teaching of computer skills) have already transitioned to a point where rote learning at home coupled with hands-on work in class is the norm.[27] For such tech-savvy educators, MOOCs are just one of many content sources available for professors to leverage as they perform their own experiments in re-engineering education.

But there is another challenge to the flipping strategy if it is to expand beyond a few early adopters: figuring out what creative exercises, group projects, and other activities are supposed to fill up all the free time that's been created by moving the lecture component of a course outside the classroom. Within many institutions there are likely to be teachers comfortable with experimentation who are eager to double or triple the amount of time spent in discussion with their students, teachers who are happy to create and share interesting classroom exercises that can fill up the hours previously taken up by lecturing. But in order for any educational transformation to grow beyond acceptance by such atypical users, there needs to be an infrastructure in place that can provide teachers/professors who are already teaching successfully using traditional classroom lectures with the resources and encouraging models that might inspire them to try something new.

And as good as the flipped classroom might be in many situations, it is likely not to be suitable for all (possibly even most) subjects, teachers, or students, in which case, current efforts to encourage this type of teaching should be treated as just another set of experiments we can learn from as SPOCs, flipping, and other technology-enabled pedagogies are put to the test in the real world.

Before leaving the topic of pedagogical experimentation, it is important to keep in mind that technology-based innovation is just one area where educational experimentation is flourishing. Outcomes-based learning, authentic assessment, hands-on instruction, and other forms of educational experimentation are being tried and implemented not just in formal school environments but within after-school enrichment programs and nontraditional learning environments such as a diversifying home-schooling movement. And while a discussion of each of these important subjects is beyond the scope of this book, educational technology making news (including MOOCs) should be thought of as part of a wider experimental culture in education.

The Origins of the MOOC Experimental Culture

Even with the spirit of academia and altruism, speculation and commerce imbuing various aspects of the MOOC project, the devotion to research and experimentation described in this chapter owes a great deal to the laboratory culture from which so many founders of MOOC companies emerged.

Sebastian Thrun, the founder of Udacity, as well as both Daphne Koller and Andrew Ng, who founded Coursera, are all computer scientists. And Anant Agarwal, president of edX, and Sanjay Sarma, MIT's director of digital learning, are both engineers. Engineering talent was required to create the technology that allows hundreds of thousands of people a day to access the multiple complex components of courses teaching different subjects in different ways. And even as MOOC course catalogs expand, remember that the first courses that drew numbers in the 100,000+ range were in computer science and engineering, with technology still being one of the top draws to MOOC-based education.

The culture of experimentation found in the scientist's and engineer's lab or the programmer's development shop represents more than just a second-nature acceptance of a scientific method requiring hypothesis testing, the collection of evidence, and the willingness to have theories proven wrong. It also requires a certain type of optimism that assumes any challenge can be overcome with enough thinking and tinkering combined with a readiness to accept (even welcome) rather than punish mistakes. This helps to explain why successes and failures in one MOOC course so quickly inform other projects, why professors in classics or Asian history can be seen sitting with statisticians and computer programmers in MOOC development meetings, and why academics who may have spent much of their careers navigating even small ideas through endless committee debates are startled when they immerse themselves in the rapid, seat-of-the-pants world of MOOC creation.

But the engineer's can-do attitude needs to continue to be balanced by all of the other experiences going into the creation of this new form of learning—especially those of veteran educators. For it is the synthesis of all of this knowledge and experience combined with the willingness to put the results of interdisciplinary collaboration to work that can ultimately set MOOCs apart from other forms of teaching—no matter how big (even massive), open, or online these other forms of teaching might be. And given that the final results of the overall MOOC experiment are likely to demonstrate that massive open learning is good (even great) in some situations and bad (or even terrible) in others, the academic drive for answers combined with the scientist's readiness to accept and even celebrate negative results should be used to guide MOOCs to the point where they can have the greatest positive impact.

THE FUTURE OF MOOCS

As the manuscript for this book was being completed, a major story making education news was the decision by Sebastian Thrun, founder and CEO of the MOOC pioneer Udacity, to "pivot" the company from his original vision of remaking the entire higher education system toward a more modest goal of training people for job readiness.[1] This decision touched off a round of schadenfreude-laced commentary, such as a piece entitled "The King of the MOOCs Abdicates the Throne" by Slate educational commentator Rebecca Schuman,[2] who used Udacity's change of course to declare the MOOC experiment a failure with high drop-out rates and enrollment demographics demonstrating that "MOOCs reify, rather than break down, privilege barriers, and as such they are not the disruptive solution their hagiographers insisted they were."

Schuman's editorial can be seen as a distillation of the indictments directed against massive open online courses by segments of the academy, with an added dynamic of MOOCs seeming to serve as a surrogate for broader criticism of efforts to reform education via technology and partnerships between the public and private sectors. And even if we take a more balanced view of issues like MOOC attrition, based on information described in chapter 4 that demonstrates that neither huge enrollment numbers nor high drop-out percentages are appropriate metrics for measuring their success or failure, there is continuing and legitimate concern over how far MOOCs or any other technology-based educational solution should be allowed to impinge on existing educational structures.

As seriously as we need to take these critiques, we also need to keep in mind that the characterization of MOOCs as part of an attempted takeover of education by Silicon Valley entrepreneurs and venture capitalists fails to take into account the large numbers of traditional educators deeply involved with the MOOC project, which means the real debate about the efficacy of massive open learning is taking place within the academy. The fact that MOOC organizations continue to fight to keep their courses free and open to all should demonstrate that their altruistic missions are not a cover for educational profiteering. Similarly, the support for technology in the classroom shown by many MOOC opponents should dispel the notion that their prime motivation is fear of the changes EdTech might bring to the traditional academy. In fact, a better starting point would take into account that both sides in the debate over MOOCs agree on the challenges facing education—skyrocketing costs, increasing class sizes, diminishing performance, lack of access—even if they propose different ways to solve them.

As Udacity's "pivot" demonstrates, the people and organizations we talk about today when we discuss MOOCs may not be the same ones who dominate the conversation in the future, presuming MOOCs have the staying power to still be worth discussing in the context of education and educational reform years from now. But regardless of whether many, some, or few of their potential futures outlined in this chapter come to be, MOOCs have already demonstrated an enormous global appetite for high-quality, college-level courses and have succeeded in triggering a transformation within institutions of higher learning where schools are now eagerly sharing assets that once might have been kept locked inside ivied bunkers. Like the technology that allows thousands to learn simultaneously, these social and institutional changes are genies that cannot easily be stuffed back into bottles, which makes answering questions regarding who will make use of these new tools and how they will use them central to understanding the potential futures of massive open learning.

College Age Learners

During the early euphoria surrounding MOOCs, a number of commentators clearly saw them as an alternative (and direct challenge) to traditional colleges and universities that were becoming increasingly expensive and decreasingly demanding, part of a higher education system that was failing to deliver the long-term economic advantages often used to justify the ever-larger investments needed to earn a diploma.

This is a critique that long predates the MOOC phenomenon. As you read in earlier chapters, programs like the Thiel Fellowship (which pays students $100,000 to not go to college) or Dale Stephen's Uncollege (which trains students on how to substitute self-study, personal experience, and mentorship for formal education), as well as different proposed variants for "hacking education," are all trying to use new educational choices (many enabled by technology) to construct less expensive yet educationally fulfilling alternatives to a formal degree. So with regard to traditional college-age learners, MOOCs were simply the latest proposed antidote for a perceived crisis in higher education that was leading to the creation of ever-larger armies of debt-laden and unemployable college graduates.

Like the blind men trying to describe an elephant, however, most of those celebrating or condemning MOOCs for what they might do to institution-based higher education programs were drawing from their own limited experience when considering what was meant by "institution-based higher education" or the alternatives proposed as a substitute. As mentioned previously, many of the policymakers and journalists covering the MOOC story spent four years between the ages of 18 and 22 attending residential (often prestigious) colleges, which gave free MOOC courses created by those name-brand schools instant cachet. But it also formed a vision for what constituted the college experience these new tools promised (or threatened) to replace. Lost in this analysis was an understanding that four years away from home in a protected academic environment describes barely half of today's college students. Decades of prioritizing higher education for all who want it has led to huge expansions of state and community college systems, many of them commuter schools. And with the growth of online programs, the percentage of students experiencing college far removed from lecture halls and dorm rooms has grown even larger. A different but equally narrow vision affects the technology entrepreneurs who have dedicated themselves to remaking education, such as Peter Thiel, founder of the Thiel Fellowship program, or Sebastian Thrun, founder of Udacity, whose Silicon Valley experience includes college dropouts becoming celebrated billionaires, teenagers selling products they invented or companies they founded for millions, and high-paying jobs flowing to skilled programmers—regardless of where (or whether) they went to school.

But even as educational programs inspired by high-tech success stories attracted entrepreneurially motivated students, they failed to take into account that such students are outliers, even within the worlds of business and technology.

Unlike programs trying to create radical alternatives to a degree obtained at a brick-and-mortar college or university, MOOCs are actually replicating a component of what is delivered at those institutions—courses—which they make freely available to all. And as those who hoped or feared that these free courses would undermine institutional learning discovered, courses alone—no matter their quantity or quality—are not enough to replace everything that goes into a degree program. But if a belief that MOOCs would completely replace residential college was short lived, the ultimate home for massive online learning among younger learners may end up being alongside existing mainstream options for obtaining college credit such as AP (which has been assigning college credit for high school work since the 1950s), CLEP (the college board's credit-by-exam program) or the type of credit-transfer opportunities facilitated by organizations like the American Council on Education described in chapter 4. In addition to these established programs, MOOCs are entering a marketplace that is filling with new credit-awarding opportunities such as the courses offered by Straighterline, a company that provides online first- and second-year general education classes that partner schools such as Western Governors

Four years away from home in a protected academic environment describes barely half of today's college students.

University and SUNY Empire State College will accept toward a four-year degree.[3]

The growth of these options fits into a larger story of students increasingly veering away from the educational calendar that characterized their parents' college experiences. For example, gap year programs in which students defer college to do something else during the year after high school are becoming increasingly popular in the United States and are already the preferred choice for 7 percent of students heading toward college in the United Kingdom.[4] And as the number of students taking time off during college or spending a year or more studying abroad also increases, college continues to transform into something other than the chance to move through four years of schooling in the same location alongside one's age cohort. Given such changes, Wesleyan president Michael Roth's vision of earning a BA in "three marvelous years" (mentioned in chapter 4) seems less a radical step and more a natural evolution of changes already underway in the diversification of what it means to "attend college."

Dr. Mohammad H. Qayoumi, president of San Jose State University, moved beyond the theoretical when he proposed mechanisms for reworking the workflow of postsecondary schooling in his white paper entitled "Reinventing Public Higher Education: A Call to Action."[5] With the familiar litany of problems in higher education as a backdrop, the paper provides specific recommendations for how to eliminate inefficiencies in credit-transfer programs and leverage new technology tools to solve problems such as classroom overcrowding, performance, and retention issues. And given San Jose State's central role in almost every MOOC experiment (and controversy), President Qayoumi is clearly ready to take chances with the new educational alternatives being built in SJSU's Silicon Valley backyard.

Understandably, educators have expressed concerns over the quality, consistency, and academic rigor of the growing number of alternatives to institution-based classroom learning, pointing out how uncontrolled diversification could end up watering down the educational and economic value of a diploma. "Diploma mill," a term that describes for-profit entities providing questionable degrees through unaccredited institutions, is increasingly becoming a pejorative directed at any degree program that places minimal demands on students. And if complaints that these newer alternative educational experiences might be lightweight, undemanding, and lacking in intimacy and security sound familiar, that is because they are the same criticisms directed against MOOCs. But of all the academic initiatives just described, only MOOCs are being developed to fulfill the needs of something other than a mass market, which is why it was much easier for me to find online classes on *The Iliad*, Kierkegaard, Einstein's Theory of Special Relativity, and ethics in MOOC catalogs than in the product list of an organization whose central mission is to provide alternatives to 101-level classes for college freshman. Liberation from having to comply with government or institutional educational content and technology standards has also allowed participants in MOOC projects to engage in the type of bold experimentation described in chapter 5.

Such a dynamic can lead to understandable accusations of dilettantism, but this misses the key point that MOOCs unmoored from present market requirements are free to explore and create, setting new standards for course quality and serving as a laboratory for new teaching and assessment methods that can benefit developers of non-massive online courses or teachers interested in leveraging MOOC content (or just copying MOOC methodologies) when flipping their own classrooms. So even if MOOCs are not likely to ever take over the academy as passionate supporters and detractors once hoped or feared, they can play a major role in how alternative educational options already being folded into traditional schooling evolve and may even find their ultimate home among these alternatives—as one option in an expanding menu of student choices.

Older Learners

Even if large numbers of eighteen-year-olds are not gravitating toward the types of courses being offered through

MOOCs, clearly hundreds of thousands of people who share my profile (as an older learner who already has a degree) are, which raises the question of whether future development of MOOCs should be directed toward the people they were originally thought to target (traditional college students) or the people who are actually taking them (mostly educated adults).

Criticism of MOOCs based on the demographic makeup of most classes implies that the learning tools that schools and investors are spending so much time and money creating are simply one more plaything for the already well off and educated who could learn this same material on their own without the output of a MOOC experiment that does not seem to be benefiting young learners. But a critique that assumes college-level courses taken after college serve little social purpose ignores the important role that formal and informal learning plays throughout many people's lives, whether that education falls under the name of professional development, job training, or continuing education.

Many occupations, such as nursing, accounting, and teaching, require in-service professionals to continually retrain, with professional development requirements creating a perpetual need for ongoing study. Similarly, careers that require professional licensure (such as health professionals) or certification (such as IT specialists) support a vast infrastructure that delivers the kind of training needed to help (usually older) professionals prepare to pass high-stakes exams. And even in fields where professional development or licensure is not required, the ongoing education of managers and employees has become such a high priority in both the public and private sectors that a new title of chief learning officer is now a fixture in the "C suite" of highly paid executives. This has led to the creation of a multibillion-dollar training industry dedicated to educating adults in subjects ranging from management, finance, and human resource issues to the latest computer programming technologies. Given the ongoing training that has been built into many job roles during an era of globalization and rapid technological change, it is no surprise that some of the most popular MOOCs have been in subjects like computer science, or that Coursera chose to make professional development courses for teachers one of the first niches they explicitly embraced. And, as noted in the last chapter's discussion of Coursera's Signature Track program, job-seekers using MOOCs to burnish their resumes or employees needing to fulfill on-the-job training requirements are ready to complete and even pay to credentialize their MOOC learning, especially when the teaching is high quality and a certificate costs less than what someone might pay to participate in a commercial professional-development or training program on the same subject.

Clearly job-related training is not what education (particularly higher education) should be all about, but issues of "vocationalism" are ones that all school systems—including the residential college and university system—struggle with in an era when humanities departments are getting squeezed to provide more resources for popular majors such as business, environmental studies, and technology-related subjects. But while long-standing online college programs, like those offered through the University of Phoenix, focus on professional areas such as business, healthcare, and information-systems management, MOOCs are one of the few educational initiatives where institutions are *investing* in liberal arts courses and, more important, people are taking them. Michael Roth's The Modern and the Post Modern drew enrollments of tens of thousands the two times the course was offered via Coursera. And without repeating arguments over enrollment numbers and completion rates detailed in chapter 4, the invention of MOOCs resulted in thousands of people involved with that class reading the works of Rousseau, Darwin, and Flaubert within a structure modeled after Roth's existing residential college course. One can make the same argument regarding HarvardX's Ancient Greek Hero class, where the 1,400 people who earned a certificate spent months closely reading *The Iliad* and *The Odyssey*, and a percentage—likely a sizable one—of the tens of thousands who enrolled but did not earn a certificate learned something about the supposedly "dying" subject of classics by auditing or just eavesdropping on a MOOC.[6]

A 1999 study by the Organization for Economic Co-operation and Development (OECD) regarding adults and continuing education showed participation rates of 40 to 50 percent in adult learning programs by those aged 25 to 64 in the United States and Western Europe.[7] And while much of that training was job specific, the range of options that were already available to adult learners through training centers, extension schools, or community education programs in 1999 has only expanded since then. For example, in 2001 the Bernard Osher Foundation began to give grants to found learning centers specifically serving lifelong learners who were not involved with formal degree programs.[8] Today, over 100 Osher-funded Lifelong Learning Institutes allow independent (again, mostly older) learners to participate in classroom-based or group-study experiences tapping the expertise of academics associated with these college-campus-based centers. And given the popularity among older learners of not just MOOCs but of recorded lecture series, such as those offered through Apple's iTunes U or the Teaching Company's Great Courses, it would seem that the intellectual curiosity of many college graduates was not sated when we were handed a diploma at the age of twenty-two.

This large (and largely unanticipated) market may also demonstrate that MOOCs have been built around the right product for older learners: the undergraduate-level course. For if K–12 education requires a hands-on mix of

MOOCs are one of the few educational initiatives where institutions are *investing* in liberal arts courses and, more important, people are taking them.

teaching techniques to promote both acquisition of knowledge and behavioral training, and graduate school is built around the type of independent research and intimate interactivity with colleagues needed to manufacture new knowledge, undergraduate courses are where students who have already been socialized for the classroom are ready to learn from people who know more than they do. This is why things like survey courses built around sage-on-stage lecturing, still effective ways of teaching curious undergraduates, can also work for more experienced learners interested in using online tools to expose themselves to unfamiliar subjects. And even as both the traditional undergraduate classroom and the MOOC are trying to use technology to move away from dependence on didactic education methods, I and my fellow seasoned students seem to be happy being taught by experts with a flair for lecturing.

So while MOOC makers should patiently cultivate the for-credit undergraduate market in order to earn a place at the table alongside other credit-bearing programs, they are in a position now to leverage an audience of older students who have already demonstrated a large and growing interest in what MOOCs have to offer. This demographic is already playing a pedagogical role in teaching and learning that takes place within many MOOCs by contributing expertise derived from experience in differing fields to student-to-student teaching within discussion forums and other communities that form around MOOC classes. And as MOOCs begin to include more creative assignments built on some of the crowdsourcing ideas described in chapter 5, younger and older learners will end up interacting in joint, participatory learning experiences that have no corollary in the intimate physical classroom.

A targeting of niche markets within this older demographic might also unearth the elusive business models MOOC providers are desperately searching for in order to bring revenue into line with costs. As mentioned previously, Coursera's Signature Track program has brought in significantly more revenue than have experimental MOOCs-for-credit business models by (1) creating a product of interest to the majority of MOOC students (older learners) and (2) offering members within that market something with "cash value" that surpasses the price they pay to a MOOC vendor. While a $50 validated certificate is worthless for someone taking a course solely for self-improvement who can obtain an unvalidated certificate for free, it might actually be an extremely cost-effective option for students and employers looking for inexpensive alternatives to costly or inflexible professional development or training programs. And while Signature Track has generated only a fraction of the revenue MOOC companies will ultimately need to survive, it points to where those looking to build a business around massive online learning should be placing their focus: on creating programs and products that help students signal their accomplishments to important audiences (such as employers) while simultaneously educating those audiences on the value MOOC-educated employees can bring to their organizations.

Even if MOOC classroom demographics change over time in a way that creates more of a balance between younger and older students, the MOOC experiment has already benefited from the involvement of tens of thousands of highly educated professionals who have been willing to act as beta testers and provide feedback (often informed by years of experience in a variety of fields) that is being incorporated into successive iterations of massive open course development. So while the education of those without the access or money needed to attend an Ivy League college should continue to be the primary goal for those committed to massive open online learning, there is no reason why students who might already have one or more degrees (including Ivy League degrees) should not be seen as active partners, and potential underwriters, for a MOOC project with broader educational and societal purposes.

Nontraditional Learners

I spent the last few days under incoming mortar and rocket attacks, then dodging checkpoints under questionable legal status to exfiltrate a war zone to a third world air field until things settled down. I had about an hour of fairly solid Internet connectivity to be able to get the assignments done, and still managed a respectable score. This is a typical week here for me.[9]

Anyone who has attended a presentation on the subject of MOOCs will be familiar with stories like the one in the e-mail reproduced above, a note sent to Sebastian Thrun of Udacity by a student in Afghanistan in appreciation for the free AI class the student was able to take, even under the most frightful conditions. Coursera's blog is filled with similarly heartwarming tales about this Mumbai teen or that refugee from Syria's civil war succeeding in self-education under challenging circumstances. And Battushig Myanganbayar, a fifteen-year-old Mongolian high school student who graduated in the top 1 percent of students taking MITx's Circuits and Electronics MOOC (while also producing Mongolian-language videos to help his classmates working through the same course), became the poster child for the transformative potential of MOOCs when he anchored his successful application to attend MIT with his edX experience.[10]

Stories like these helped generate much of the original zeal for MOOCs as potential game-changers in global education, and while such emotional anecdotes should not shield MOOCs from legitimate criticism, the bigger story represented by these nontraditional learning experiences may be the changes wrought by MOOCs implemented in niche educational communities.

When drawing a comparison between MOOC-based and traditional education, an image frequently invoked for a MOOC student is that of a pajama-clad independent learner working in isolation in front of his or her computer screen. But when MOOCs are implemented in atypical learning environments, they are often part of a blended learning experience where students watch Udacity, Coursera, or edX lecture videos together in the same physical location (which might be a classroom, courtyard, or sports stadium) and then spend the rest of class discussing the content or working together on problem sets or group projects. Leaders of edX have described the implementation of their programs in rural areas where schools dedicate the few hours of electricity and bandwidth available each day to run equipment needed to deliver MOOC content to students, "flipping" to classroom participatory learning mode when power is no longer available. Even the archetypal story of Battushig Myanganbayar demonstrates the success of MOOCs as a component of blended learning, rather than a substitute for the classroom, given that his achievement was built from help he received from a recent Stanford graduate who visited Mongolia to act as a classroom tutor facilitating a hybrid online/hands-on learning program supported by the school's principal, Enkhmunkh Zurgaanjin (Mongolia's first graduate from MIT).

These types of learning experiences are not being considered only in places where no other means to study subjects like computer science or the humanities at the college level are available. At the 2013 Learning International Networks Consortium (LINC) conference at MIT, the leaders of virtual university programs in Africa, South America, Europe, and Asia joined with leaders of MIT and edX to reflect on what MOOCs might be able to offer— as well as learn from—established global virtual learning programs.[11] At that event, Sir John Daniel, former chancellor of the UK Open University, expressed skepticism over whether massive classes with no clear pathway toward college credit could ever supplant what virtual universities were already doing successfully (albeit not for free). In contrast, Dr. Patricio López del Puerto, president of the Virtual University of the Tecnológico de Monterrey in Monterrey, Mexico (a school already offering over 2,000 courses to over 20,000 academic students and over 140,000 students in corporate training programs across Latin America), saw MOOCs as part of a broad range of advances in educational technology being embraced by school systems that must balance enormous need with limited resources.

The long list of challenges these school systems face, "digital divide" power, bandwidth and technical experience limitations, huge populations needing to be educated, lack of trained teachers (not to the mention poverty, illiteracy, and political instability affecting education in many parts of the world), cannot be solved by a few hundred hugely enrolled online courses, most of them delivered in English.

But people trying to close the digital divide or fight poverty through education do not look at MOOCs as poor substitutes for four years at Princeton. Rather, they see them as godsends more than worth the effort required to come up with workarounds for their current limitations. And those workarounds should not simply be seen as local "hacks" of no significance beyond such challenging educational environments. For the blended learning models being pioneered in many Third World locations are inspiring the creation of similar MOOC experiments elsewhere through programs such as Coursera's learning hubs that encourage the use of MOOC content within flipped or blended learning classes anchored to physical locations such as US embassies. And in the United States, where the value of virtual vs. residential education continues to be hotly debated, a creative program designed to hybridize various learning modalities is MOOC Campus: a college without a faculty where students participate in a residential educational experiment where MOOCs, mentors and student-colleagues work together in a "self-organized learning environment" (SOLE).[12] That acronym is actually attached to the umbrella program for MOOC Campus—Black Mountain SOLE—which was established on the site of Black Mountain College, one of the most famous experiments in alternative higher education, which ran from 1933 to 1957. And while it is unclear how big a role MOOCs will play in this new incarnation of Black Mountain, they are already creating an opportunity for one experimental institution to radically redefine what we mean when we use the word "college."

Of all the futures for MOOCs described in this chapter, their implementation in parts of the world where they represent the best hope for affordable, high-quality education may have the most promise for triggering the kind of revolutionary change envisioned when MOOCs first burst into public consciousness. Distance educators talk about nations such as India being able to leapfrog the building of expensive, difficult-to-staff residential colleges for the hundreds of thousands of Indian students seeking higher education in favor of robust virtual universities, in the way that many developing countries leapt right to cellular telecommunications, skipping over landline technology entirely. And even in the United States, administrators and facilities planners overseeing building projects on expanding college campuses are starting to consider whether additional lecture halls will be needed if flipped classrooms and blended courses (whether powered by MOOCs or other forms of digital content) create the need for more labs and intimate spaces facilitating group discussion, mentoring, and both student-to-teacher and student-to-student interaction. Beyond their pure altruistic purposes, the use of MOOCs in nontraditional educational settings may actually provide revenue opportunities for MOOC vendors able to tap funds from governments or nongovernment organizations (NGOs) focusing on education.

And for those holding out hope for MOOCs as a genuinely transformational technology, these atypical educational niches should also be seen as potential launch pads for the type of widespread disruption of the academy originally envisioned when MOOCs first made an appearance on the educational landscape.

Disruptive Technology

In his 2008 book *Disrupting Class*, Professor Clayton Christensen from Harvard Business School and coauthors Michael Horn and Curtis Johnson applied models they created to describe how industries are disrupted to the field of education.[13]

Contrary to the intuitive notion of a new invention kicking older products out of the marketplace as a result of lower cost or technical superiority, the disruptive technologies Christensen looks at actually entered markets with severe shortcomings compared to existing mainstream choices. His archetypal case is the personal computer, a product built and brought to market by a collection of hobbyists and garage-based entrepreneurs that was scoffed at by the manufacturers of "real" computers, that is, the mainframe and minicomputers being bought by governments, corporations, universities, and other institutions to manage programs like the US census or global airline scheduling. Such customers were not asking IBM or Digital Equipment Corporation for underpowered toys that connected to nothing, but for bigger, faster, and more powerful machines for which they would continue paying top dollar. But as microcomputers drew little to no interest from traditional computer buyers (institutions who continued to purchase "big iron"), they found new customers in different markets: home and small business users who could not afford even the cheapest minicomputer and would have no idea what to do with it if they bought one. And these markets turned out to be big enough not just to create a parallel computer industry but to support investment in innovation needed to allow PC and then PC-networking technologies to evolve to a point where they were able to disrupt the once scoffing "big iron" manufacturers out of existence.

In *Disrupting Class*, Christensen was primarily looking at how technology (specifically pre-MOOC online learning tools) could affect the public school system. Unlike many critics, Christensen was actually impressed at how US public schools managed to meet every challenge asked of them, from inculcating democratic values, to providing options for every student, to keeping the country competitive and fighting poverty. But such a system was always built around a structure that required students in the same age cohort and living in the same geographical location to learn the same subjects at the same time. And as much as the public school system has evolved to support the needs of individual students, institution-based learning is still founded on the simultaneous education of groups, with limited ability to focus on the specific requirements of individuals with different interests, abilities (which can range dramatically between subjects), and learning styles. So for Christensen, the most powerful aspect of technology is the ability it gives educators to tailor learning to each student's unique needs.

As with microcomputers, the first online courses were clearly inferior to teaching delivered in the classroom. And when making a one-to-one comparison between a MOOC course and the same course being given in an intimate classroom environment, most people would point to the classroom as providing a superior overall learning experience (even if they might choose to participate in the MOOC for reasons of convenience). But convenience is not the only reason to take part in a HarvardX MOOC rather than taking the same class at Harvard. For example, Harvard accepts only approximately 2,000 students (primarily eighteen-year-olds) per year into its undergraduate program, which leaves everyone older or younger than that age, everyone who cannot get into or afford to attend Harvard, and everyone living in parts of the world with no access to the university with no other choice but to take the MOOC if they want access to that course. And whether we are talking about older continuing education students watching lecture videos in the basement or Nigerian kids gathering in a football stadium to participate together in a MOOC-powered blended learning program, "no other choice" translates to access to never-before-available educational opportunity.

Perhaps this is why new MOOC classes continue to draw tens of thousands of students despite everything that has been written about their alleged inferiority to "real" college learning. For students of any age eager enough to work their way through challenging subjects like circuit design or Greek literature are more than likely up to the task of living with or working around the limitations MOOCs have in areas such as assessment, discussion, and lack of "signal" to employers. More important, it is in just those "no other alternative" niches that disruptive innovation emerges. Individuals interested in having a computer in their home, classroom, or office in the early days of PCs had no choice other than to buy a clunky Apple II or fifty-pound IBM PC, and were happy to live with slow speed and other limitations no one would tolerate today. Similarly, as Christensen points out, schools have implemented online courses, even when a classroom version of such courses would probably be superior, but only in situations where such a classroom option was not possible (for example, when students express interest in taking AP classes at schools without AP-qualified instructors). And it is from these "no choice" niches that innovation develops, some of it growing out of the MOOC experimentation described in chapter 5, some of it deriving from other areas of a hot EdTech economy fueled by investors hoping that Cisco CEO John Chambers was right when he announced during his keynote for the 2001 Comdex computing conference that "E-Learning is the next killer app: it will make email look like a rounding error."

Comparing my own MOOC experiences to earlier online classes I have taken, including an expensive graduate-level class in education with fewer than twenty students, it was startling to me how much MOOCs have upped the ante in terms of production values, creativity, and risk taking. Which means that from within the various educational niches MOOCs are serving, they are already setting a new standard that other online courses will need to meet or be judged inferior to no-credit "MOOCware" that will be harder to dismiss as educationally worthless the more it continues to outshine what came before.

Even as some MOOC experiments are attempting to create more intimacy within classrooms of thousands or leverage those huge numbers to engage in educational activity that cannot be done in a "normal" physical classroom, other projects—such as those involving using MOOC content as part of blended or flipped classroom projects—are avoiding problems associated with massive open learning by treating MOOCs as just one of many content sources creative educators can use to construct their own classroom experiences that combine the best of online and hands-on learning. And, once again, it is inside educational niches—whether in rural Pakistan or on the campus of Black Mountain SOLE—that the infrastructure needed to support long-term transformation is being built.

In addition to raising the bar for online learning and providing a platform to explore new innovative classroom experiences, the emergence of MOOCs has also forced those selling the continuing value of traditional residential learning to take a closer look at what they are actually providing that might justify the ever-rising costs of attending college. And even if the initial claims that MOOCs would immediately shake the academy to its foundations turned out to be based on uninformed wishful (or fearful) thinking, the scare such claims delivered helped trigger a vital conversation over how schools can change their current hyperinflationary course lest they be overtaken by whichever wave of technical innovation manages to finally create an alternative to traditional institution-based education that gets embraced by the mainstream.

There is always the possibility that MOOCs will turn out to be a fad (or, in modern parlance, a "transitional technology"), or interest in sustaining investment in their continuing development might fade (especially if no workable business model emerges that can allow them to become financially viable). And if we continue to think of MOOCs as nothing more than big, free classes offered by talented professors from generous schools, then perhaps they might face the same fate as AllLearn or the many Internet businesses that thought they could give desirable things away for free and figure out how to make money later. But if MOOCs continue to embrace—or even expand on—the culture of experimentation and innovation that has already set them apart from nearly all other adventures in technology-based learning, if they continue to offer high-quality free teaching to the world while also serving as the laboratory where educational innovation thrives, then whatever MOOCs are today or whatever they evolve into, they are likely to leave an important mark on whatever ends up being called higher education in the future.

As I mentioned at the start of this book, the "final exam" for my Degree of Freedom One Year BA project consisted of attending the 2013 Eastern Division Conference of the American Philosophical Association (APA) in Baltimore, Maryland, where over 1,000 philosophy professors and graduate students gathered to give papers, discuss the field, and party and refute one another into the night at evening "smokers."

That trip was meant to help answer one of the questions that came up frequently as I was finishing up my informal philosophy degree: whether or not MOOCs and other forms of free learning could ever provide the same level of education as what someone would receive by attending a traditional residential college program. As you have read in this book, it is not difficult to determine if an individual MOOC comes close to paralleling a semester-long conventional course: some try and succeed, some try and fall short, and some were created to do things other than replicate what takes place in a traditional college classroom. But can insights regarding the rigor and scope of the 30+ individual courses taken over the course of a year be summed to establish the worth of that overall learning experience?

Having studied philosophy, my first instinct is to present both sides of the argument.

Starting with the prosecution, when I was first planning out a curriculum for my One Year BA, I did some rough research to see if it might be possible to squeeze four years' worth of courses into one year at a residential college. Unsurprisingly, no school calendar I could find would allow someone to fit this many classes into such a short period of time. But as a year of taking online courses dredged up memories of what was involved with getting through similar classes when I originally went to college, it was clear that even if logistics could be made to work, trying to fit 32 semester-long, brick-and-mortar college classes into twelve months would not be possible given the workload of courses created by professors who assume their students are each taking no more than 4 or 5 classes at a time. This would imply that if a program (like my One Year BA) allowed me to complete that many courses in one year rather than four, then the online courses I took must—on average—be easier than the ones someone would go through in a traditional four-year BA program. And if you totaled up the hours of lectures watched, papers written, and exam questions answered over the course of my twelve-month project, it would be hard to argue that this workload was comparable to what someone is asked to do over eight college semesters.

But arguing for the defense, should we be basing who had a "real" college experience and who did not on metrics such as number of lectures attended and pages read and written, or should success in higher education be determined based on what a student becomes as a result of the experience?

For example, if I asked everyone reading this book to write up a list of all the classes you took in college, I suspect that most of you would come up with rough names for about half the courses you once sweated over. And speaking of sweat, what might happen if I asked you to retake the final exam from one of those classes, let's say the same final you passed with flying colors when you first took the course? If visions of panic and Fs are flashing through your head, does that indicate you really did not learn anything in those courses you spent so much money to have access to and so much time and effort trying to pass? Probably not, since if you had a week to prepare for that test (or to write a paper summarizing the key points in a class) you could probably brush up on the material, drawing from sources now widely available on the Internet and synthesizing that content with an a priori understanding of key concepts you developed when you first took the course.

Having studied chemistry when I went to college years ago, I was trained to think like a chemist and, as part of that training, as a scientist (just as my wife, who studied history as an undergraduate and later went on to earn a

PhD in the subject, has been trained think like a historian). And for anyone now working in the field they studied while in college, the specifics they learned are probably ready-to-hand, especially if they have been put to work on a regular basis since graduation.

This thought experiment is meant to point out the irony inherent in the fact that while we think we know a great deal because of our college degree, when it comes right down to it we really know nothing. Which means that as we evaluate not just MOOCs but any alternative forms of higher education, we need to compare them to a residential college experience whose main intellectual benefit was not the classes we took or assignments we performed (most of which we can barely remember) but what that experience turned us into.

So rather than evaluate my One Year BA experience based on the length and rigor of the courses I completed, what would happen if we instead looked at the transformative effects studying a degree's worth of material might have had on this student?

As a philosophy major I now have enough of a grasp on modern philosophical concepts such as *a priori knowledge* (Kant), *ready-to-hand* (Heidegger), and *irony* (Kierkegaard) to make use of them in the analysis you have just been reading. And these and other subjects (about which I knew nothing twelve months ago) have been internalized to a point where they informed a year of analysis of the subject of MOOCs and free learning, including many passages in this book. Now the ability to use philosophical ideas in such a way hardly makes me a philosopher. But might it be fair to consider myself the equivalent of a graduating senior with a BA in philosophy who is now capable of applying important philosophical principles to different subjects and different aspects of life?

While I joked with friends that my final grade for my One Year BA would be based on whether or not I felt like an idiot sitting through the half-dozen APA sessions I planned to attend, it became clear fairly quickly that my year-long learning adventure had more than prepared me to follow along with everything being presented and even participate intelligently in discussions. No doubt any of the PhDs at the conference could crush me in a refutation duel as easily as they could drink me under the table at the evening smoker. But dozens of online courses, including MOOCs from some of the best universities in the world, had managed to turn me into something I was not just twelve short months ago. As Professor Jeffrey Pomerantz from UNC (whom you met in chapter 4) might put it: *contemplate that*.

GLOSSARY

Accreditation
Review of a course, program, school, or other educational institution or component, usually performed by a third-party, to ensure adherence to a set of predetermined standards. In a few cases, MOOCs have been accredited by a third party (such as the American Council on Education) in a way that allows students to gain college credit for passing an accredited course. (See chapter 4.)

Auditing
Enrolling and participating in a course without taking it for a grade. This might involve sitting through lectures and doing assigned reading, but not taking exams or submitting written work.

Blended learning
A mode of teaching that mixes classroom and online delivery of course materials. This might include lectures delivered by online video, discussion facilitated by blogs and or online forums, or submission of papers and other graded assignments via an online learning management system.

cMOOC
Acronym for Connectivist Massive Open Online Course, specifying a large-scale, open enrollment online course based on the principles of connectivism. (See chapter 2.)

Connectivism
A theory of teaching and learning modeled on how the human brain works that associates new knowledge with a net gain in neural connections. When applied to online classes, connectivist models are sometimes referred to as "networked learning." (See chapter 2.)

Crowdsourcing
A centrally directed effort leveraging large groups of people, facilitated via the Internet. (See chapter 5 for some examples of crowdsourced assignments given within MOOC classes.)

Curation
In the context of free-learning, curation is the collection of educational material from sources like the open web in order to create courses or support the learning that takes place inside a residential or online class.

EdTech
An abbreviation for "educational technology."

Fair use doctrine
A legal principle that governs when copyrighted material may be used for educational or journalistic purposes without requiring licensing or permission from the copyright owner.

Flipped classroom
A form of blended learning in which students watch video recordings of a professor's lectures as homework, then use class time for extended discussion or work on projects (such as problem sets) that might have historically been assigned as homework.

Free learning
A catch-all term for various free educational resources, which can include MOOCs, recorded lectures from sources such as iTunes U, educational podcasts, and curated courses that leverage some or all of the free educational material available on the World Wide Web.

Gap year
An increasingly popular choice by students to defer college enrollment in order to spend the year between high school and college pursuing other opportunities such as travel or independent learning.

Learning management system (LMS)
Online systems that automate the interaction between students, teachers and administrators at an educational institution.

Meet-up
The use of online tools to facilitate people with a common interest finding one another to organize a physical meeting. Most MOOC systems provide meet-up functionality that allows students taking the same class to find one another in order to form a study group. (See chapter 3.)

MOOC
An acronym for massive open online course. (See chapter 3 for a detailed discussion for how a MOOC might be defined.)

Open access
A licensing arrangement that allows scholars and researchers to share articles and results outside the traditional framework of distribution through commercial academic publishers. (See chapter 4.)

Open educational resources (OER)
Educational content (such as syllabi, lecture videos or notes, reading lists, tests, and paper assignments) provided for free use by educators. MIT's OpenCourse-Ware initiative is currently the best-known OER initiative. (See chapter 1.)

Peer grading
A method for grading papers or other subjective assignments whereby students grade one another's work, normally using detailed rubrics provided by an instructor.

Rubric
A set of instructions on how an assignment (such as a written paper or in-class observed activity) should be graded that provides criteria for scoring and specific instructions of what a student needs to do to meet each criterion. (See chapter 3.)

SPOC
An acronym for small private online class, which has been used to refer to a MOOC with restricted enrollment as well as flipped classrooms where MOOCs may provide one or more components of an existing residential course. (See chapter 5.)

xMOOC
A term used to describe MOOCs that tend to follow the same structure as a traditional residential college class to distinguish them from cMOOCs, which are designed around the nontraditional principles of connectivism. (See chapter 2.)

NOTES

Preface

1. See Thomas L. Friedman, "Come the Revolution," *New York Times*, May 16, 2012, p. A25, available at http://www.nytimes.com/2012/05/16/opinion/friedman-come-the-revolution.html; "Revolution Hits the Universities," *New York Times*, January 27, 2013, p. SR1, available at http://www.nytimes.com/2013/01/27/opinion/sunday/friedman-revolution-hits-the-universities.html; and "The Professor's Big Stage," *New York Times*, March 6, 2013, p. A23, available at http://www.nytimes.com/2013/03/06/opinion/friedman-the-professors-big-stage.html.

2. See Steven Leckart, "The Stanford Education Experiment Could Change Higher Learning Forever," *Wired* 20, no. 4 (April 2012): 68, available at http://www.wired.com/2012/03/ff_aiclass/.

3. The web site I created to document this experience, www.degreeoffreedom.org, contains reflections and analysis on the MOOC story as well as course reviews and interviews with leaders in the MOOC movement.

Chapter 1

1. See Laura Pappano, "The Year of the MOOC," *New York Times*, November 4, 2012, p. ED26, available at http://www.nytimes.com/2012/11/04/education/edlife/massive-open-online-courses are-multiplying-at-a-rapid-pace.html.

2. MIT still has the most expansive catalog of OpenCourseWare resources, available at http://ocw.mit.edu/index.htm. There is also a global OpenCourse-Ware Consortium whose membership list and resources are available at http://www.ocwconsortium.org/.

3. See Steve Kolowich, "Why Some Colleges Are Saying No to MOOC Deals, at Least for Now," *Chronicle of Higher Education* 59, no. 34 (May 3, 2013), available at http://chronicle.com/article/Why-Some-Colleges-Are-Saying/138863/.

4. See Steve Kolowich, "Professor Leaves a MOOC in Mid-Course in Dispute over Teaching," *Wired Campus—Chronicle of Higher Education* (blog), February 18, 2013, available at http://chronicle.com/blogs/wiredcampus/professor-leaves-a-mooc-in-mid-course-in-dispute-over-teaching/42381.

5. See "An Open Letter to Professor Michael Sandel from the Philosophy Department at San Jose State University," *Chronicle of Higher Education* (online), May 2, 2013, available at http://chronicle.com/article/The-Document-an-Open-Letter/138937/.

6. See Marc Parry, "A Star MOOC Professor Defects—at Least for Now," *Chronicle of Higher Education* 60, no. 02 (September 3, 2013), available at http://chronicle.com/article/A-MOOC-Star-Defects-at-Least/141331/.

7. Information on Gartner's Hype Cycle research and methodology can be found at http://www.gartner.com/technology/research/methodologies/hype-cycle.jsp.

Chapter 2

1. See Diane Matthews, "The Origins of Distance Education," *T H E Journal [Technological Horizons in Education]* 27, no. 2 (September 1999): 54, available at http://thejournal.com/articles/1999/09/01/the-origins-of-distance-education-and-its-use-in-the-united-states.aspx.

2. The organization still exists and continues to offer mail-based correspondence instruction in studio art under its current name of Art Instruction Schools (www.artinstructionschools.edu/).

3. See Michael Grahame Moore, "From Chautauqua to the Virtual University: A Century of Distance Education in the United States," *ERIC Clearinghouse on Adult, Career, and Vocational Education*, Columbus, OH (2003), available at http://files.eric.ed.gov/fulltext/ED482357.pdf.

4. While door-to-door booksellers would eventually come to be associated with the sale of encyclopedias, the American novelist Mark Twain used this method as his primary means of getting his works into the hands—and money out of the pockets—of American readers.

5. For more information on early education-by-broadcast initiatives, see "A Brief History of Distance Education" by Bizhan Nasseh of Ball State University, available at http://www.seniornet.org/edu/art/history.html.

6. Open University (http://www.open.ac.uk/), which continues to be one of the world's largest providers of distance learning, created its own MOOC spinoff in 2013 called FutureLearn (https://www.futurelearn.com/), which provides access to free MOOC classes created by UK universities such as Kings College and the University of Edinburgh.

7. See B.F. Skinner, "Why We Need Teaching Machines," *Harvard Educational Review* 31 (1961): 377–398.

8. See Mary Timmins, "In the Time of Plato," *Illinois Alumni Magazine*, September 10, 2010, available at http://www.uiaa.org/illinois/news/blog/comments.asp?id=163. A PLATO History web site is also available at http://platohistory.org.

9. See Kim Parker, Amanda Lenhart, and Kathleen Moore, "The Digital Revolution and Higher Education," *Pew Internet and American Life Project*, August 28, 2011, available at http://www.pewinternet.org/2011/08/28/the-digital-revolution-and-higher-education/.

10. See Jeffrey R. Young, "When Professors Print Their Own Diplomas, Who Needs Universities?," *Chronicle of Higher Education* 55, no. 6 (October 3, 2008), available at http://chronicle.com/article/When-Professors-Print-Their/1185/.

11. Stephen Downes, who runs the popular site Stephen's Web (www.downes .ca) has self-published a book on the connectivist philosophy of teaching and learning which is available for free download at http://www.downes.ca/post/58207.

12. You can hear an EdTechTalk interview with Siemens and Downes at http://edtechtalk.com/EdTechTalk81.

13. For a discussion of the flipped classroom, see Tina Rosenberg, "Turning Education Upside Down," *New York Times*, Opinionator (blog), October 9, 2013, available at http://opinionator.blogs.nytimes.com/2013/10/09/turning-education-upside-down/?_r=0, and "In 'Flipped' Classrooms, a Method for Mastery," *New York Times*, Opinionator (blog), October 23, 2013, available at http://opinionator.blogs.nytimes.com/2013/10/23/in-flipped-classrooms-a-method-for-mastery/.

14. Two books which look at the cost crisis in higher education from different perspectives include *Tuition Rising: Why College Costs So Much* by Ronald G. Ehrenberg (Cambridge, MA: Harvard University Press, 2002) and *Why Does College Cost So Much?* by Ronert B. Archibald and David H. Feldman (Oxford: Oxford University Press, 2010).

Chapter 3

1. Donald A. Bligh, *What's the Use of Lectures?* (New York: Jossey-Bass, 2000).

2. See Salman Kahn, "Why Long Lectures Are Ineffective," *Time Magazine*, October 2, 2012, available at http://ideas.time.com/2012/10/02/why-lectures-are-ineffective/.

3. See John F. Wakefield, "A Brief History of Textbooks: Where Have We Been All These Years?," paper presented at the Meeting of the Text and Academic Authors (1998), available at http://files.eric.ed.gov/fulltext/ED419246.pdf.

4. For a detailed discussion of open access, see *Open Access* by Peter Suber (Cambridge, MA: MIT Press, 2012).

5. See chapter 5 for examples of the publishing industry's business-model experimentation in the MOOC market.

6. Richard Arum and Josipa Roska, *Academically Adrift—Limited Learning on College Campuses* (Chicago: University of Chicago Press, 2011).

7. See Dr. Katrina A. Meyer, "Face to Face vs. Threaded Discussion: The Role of Time and Higher-Order Thinking," *Journal of Asynchronous Learning Networks (JALN)* 7, no. 3 (2003): 55–65, available at http://sloanconsortium.org/sites/default/files/v7n3_meyer_1.pdf.

8. See Olla Najah Al-Shalchi, "The Effectiveness and Development of Online Discussions," *Journal of Online Teaching and Learning* 5, no. 1 (March 2009), available at http://jolt.merlot.org/vol5no1/al-shalchi_0309.htm.

9. See Jeffrey R. Young, "What a Tech Start-Up's Data Say about What Works in Classroom Forums," *The Chronicle of Higher Education* (blog), August 21, 2012, available at http://chronicle.com/blogs/wiredcampus/what-a-tech-start-ups-data-say-about-what-works-in-classroom-forums/38960?cid=at&utm_source=at&utm_medium=en.

10. Writer A. J. Jacobs, author of *The Year of Living Biblically* (Simon & Schuster, 2008) included a description of his failed attempts to meet up with fellow students in New York in a lighthearted *New York Times* opinion piece chronicling his taking of eleven MOOC classes (two of which he completed): A. J. Jacobs, "Two Cheers for Web U!," *New York Times*, April 21, 2013, available at http://www.nytimes.com/2013/04/21/opinion/sunday/grading-the-mooc-university.html. This author can confirm similar lack of success in trying to get study groups off the ground in the Boston area.

11. For a description of how different types of testing are used in education, see chapters 7–12 of *NETS*S: Resources for Student Assessment* by M. G. (Peggy) Kelly and Jon Haber, published by the International Society for Technology in Education (2006).

12. See Tamar Lewin, "College of Future Could Be Come One, Come All," *New York Times*, November 20, 2012, p. A1, available at http://www.nytimes.com/2012/11/20/education/colleges-turn-to-crowd-sourcing-courses.html?pagewanted=1&_r=2.

13. As an example of one of the confounding factors that can be introduced in an uncontrolled grading environment, when I peer-graded student essays I tended to be lenient with any student who identified that English was not his or her primary language. Multiply this ad hoc policy by the personal choices of other unsupervised and untrained graders and you can see how much subjectivity can creep into peer-grading processes based on even the most well-designed scoring rubrics.

14. Kelly and Haber, *Resources for Student Assessment*, chapters 10–11.

15. As a demonstration that this liberation from the semester does not necessarily lead only to shorter courses, at the end of 2013 those of us enrolled in HarvardX's *History of China* learned that the course would be broken into a series of modules released over fifteen months.

16. See Steven Leckart, "The Stanford Education Experiment Could Change Higher Learning Forever," *Wired*, March 20, 2012, available at http://www.wired.com/wiredscience/2012/03/ff_aiclass/all/.

17. For example, a HarvardX *Neuroscience* class taught by Professor David Cox provides students the chance to perform experiments using a lab kit that costs $100. While participating in such experimentation does not contribute to a grade, a student who can afford one of these kits is likely to have a superior experience with the course than someone who cannot. (See chapter 5 for a description of a fundraising campaign Professor Cox used to raise money for students who wanted to participate in class experiments but could not afford the apparatus.).

18. Harvard restricted enrollments for its CopyrightX MOOC to 500 to facilitate organized small group discussion and allow for teacher/teaching-assistant grading of assignments.

19. In fact, while this book was being written, the MOOC pioneer Udacity announced a "pivot" away from public education and toward corporate training (discussed further in chapter 6). But given that this business decision was not accompanied by any changes to their free course offerings, questions over whether or not Udacity remains a MOOC vendor demonstrate the challenges facing us without an effective definition of what constitutes a MOOC.

20. In September 2013, edX and Google announced a partnership to create MOOC.org, a platform that will allow anyone to post a course using the edX open-source course management system running on Google servers, which provides yet another option for colleges and universities (or anyone else) to produce MOOC courses, bypassing today's "Big Three" MOOC vendors entirely.

21. This statement appears on the edX web site alongside a list of goals and principles underlying the edX mission, available at https://www.edx.org/about-us.

22. Daphne Koller, "What We're Learning from Online Education," *Ted Talks* recorded August 2012, available at http://www.ted.com/talks/daphne_koller_what_we_re_learning_from_online_education.html.

23. Stephen Downes, interview with author, Degree of Freedom Podcast (December 20 2013), available at http://degreeoffreedom.org/interview-stephen-downes/.

Chapter 4

1. For a critique of the MOOC critics, see James G. Mazoue, "Five Myths about MOOCs," *Educause Review Online*, October 7, 2013, available at http://www.educause.edu/ero/article/five-myths-about-moocs?utm_source=Informz&utm_medium=Emailmarketing&utm_campaign=EDUCAUSE. And for a critique of this critique, see Rollin Moe, "No Space to Debate MOOCS," *All MOOCs, All the Time* (blog), October 15, 2013, available at https://allmoocs.wordpress.com/tag/luddite/.

2. See Susan Meisenhelder, "MOOC Mania," *Thought & Action* 29 (Fall 2013): 7–23, available at http://www.nea.org/assets/docs/HE/TA2013Meisenhelder.pdf.

3. This 2013 University of Edinburgh report is available at https://www.era.lib.ed.ac.uk/bitstream/1842/6683/1/Edinburgh_MOOCs_Report2013_no1.pdf.

4. A series on Professor Pomerantz's findings is available on his personal blog, beginning at http://jeffrey.pomerantz.name/2013/11/data-about-the-metadata-mooc-part-1/.

5. See Lori Breslow, David E. Pritchard, Jennifer DeBoer, Glenda Stump, Andres Ho, and Daniel T. Seaton, "Studying Learning in the Worldwide Classroom," *Research & Practice in Assessment* 8 (Summer 2013): 13–25, available at http://www.rpajournal.com/dev/wp-content/uploads/2013/05/SF2.pdf.

6. See Pat Lopes Harris, "SJSU/EdX Adds More Campuses, Courses," *SJSU Today* (blog), April 10, 2013, available at http://blogs.sjsu.edu/today/2013/sjsuedx-expansion/.

7. See Lee Gardner and Jeffrey R. Young, "California's Move toward MOOCs Sends Shock Waves, but Key Questions Remain Unanswered," *Chronicle of Higher Education*, March 14, 2013, available at http://chronicle.com/article/California-Considers-a-Bold/137903/.

8. See Ry Rivard, "Taking on Accreditors and Faculty," *Inside Higher Ed*, April 11, 2013, available at http://www.insidehighered.com/news/2013/04/11/florida-legislation-would-require-colleges-grant-credit-some-unaccredited-courses.

9. While some schools have shown a willingness to allow different types of work experience to count toward a degree, many of the companies offering diplomas based on work or life experience alone are generally considered scams.

10. Information on the ACE CREDIT program is available at http://www.acenet.edu/news-room/Pages/College-Credit-Recommendation-Service-CREDIT.aspx.

11. A list of participating training organizations, and associated ACE credit recommended courses, is available at http://www2.acenet.edu/credit/?fuseaction=browse.main.

12. See Jay Cross, "How I Saved $30K and Graduated 1.5 Years Early by "Testing Out," Huffington Post (January 14, 2014), available at http://www.huffingtonpost.com/jay-cross/how-i-saved-30k-graduated_b_4591693.html.

13. See Steve Kolowich, "American Council on Education Recommends 5 MOOCs for Credit," *Chronicle of Higher Education* 59, no. 23 (February 15, 2013), available at http://chronicle.com/article/American-Council-on-Education/137155/.

14. See Steve Kolowich, "A University's Offer of Credit for a MOOC Gets No Takers," *The Chronicle of Higher Education*, July 8, 2013, available at http://chronicle.com/article/A-Universitys-Offer-of-Credit/140131/.

15. Information on the Thiel Fellowship program is available at http://www.thielfellowship.org/.

16. See Dale Stephens, *Hacking Your Education: Ditch the Lectures, Save Tens of Thousands, and Learn More Than Your Peers Ever Will* (New York: Perigee Trade, 2013). Also, information on Stephens's Uncollege program is available at http://www.uncollege.org/.

17. See Steve Kolowich, "California Puts MOOC Bill on Ice," *Chronicle of Higher Education*, August 1, 2013, available at http://chronicle.com/blogs/wiredcampus/california-puts-mooc-bill-on-ice/45215.

18. See "'Watered Down' MOOC Bill Becomes Law in Florida," *Inside Higher Ed*, July 1, 2013, available at http://www.insidehighered.com/quicktakes/2013/07/01/watered-down-mooc-bill-becomes-law-florida.

19. See Michael Roth, "A Degree in 'Three Marvelous Years,'" *Washington Post (College Inc. blog)*, May 23, 2012, available at http://www.washingtonpost.com/blogs/college-inc/post/wesleyan-president-a-degree-in-three-marvelous-years/2012/05/23/gJQANAIIlU_blog.html.

20. See Michael Roth, interview with author, Degree of Freedom Podcast (July 12, 2103), available at http://degreeoffreedom.org/interview-with-wesleyan-president-michael-roth-part-1-2/.

21. See Kayla Webley, "MOOC Brigade: Can Online Courses Keep Students from Cheating?," *Time Magazine*, November 19, 2012, available at http://nation.time.com/2012/11/19/mooc-brigade-can-online-courses-keep-students-from-cheating/?iid=tsmodule.

22. See Jake New, "MOOC Teaches How to Cheat in Online Courses, with Eye to Prevention," *The Chronicle of Higher Education* (blog), May 2, 2013, available

at http://chronicle.com/blogs/wiredcampus/mooc-teaches-how-to-cheat-in -online-courses-with-eye-to-prevention/43699.

23. See Donald McCabe, Linda Klebe Trevino, and Kenneth D. Butterfield, "Cheating in Academic Institutions," *Ethics & Behavior* 11, no. 3 (2001): 219– 232, available at http://faculty.mwsu.edu/psychology/dave.carlston/Writing %20in%20Psychology/Academic%20Dishonesty/Gropu%203/review.pdf.

24. Toward the end of my Degree of Freedom project, when course work was competing with the completion of this book, I found myself "hacking" homework for my last remaining class, a process that fell between dishonesty and putting in your best effort. A description of that experience is available at http:// www.huffingtonpost.com/jonathan-haber/hacking-homework_b_4461643. html.

25. Kyle Courtney, interview with author, Degree of Freedom Podcast (October 25, 2013), available at http://degreeoffreedom.org/interview-kyle-courtney-copyright-advisor-harvard-harvardx/.

26. Peter Suber, *Open Access* (Cambridge, MA: MIT Press, 2012).

27. See Sanjay Sarma and Isaac Chuang, "The Magic beyond the MOOCs," *MIT Faculty Newsletter* 25, no. 5 (May/June 2013), available at http://web.mit.edu/ fnl/volume/255/sarmay_chuang.html.

28. Anya Kamenetz, *DIY U: Edupunks, Edupreneurs, and the Coming Transformation of Higher Education* (White River Junction, VT: Chelsea Green Publishing, 2010).

Chapter 5

1. See Daphne Koller, Andrew Ng, Chuong Do, and Zhenghao Chen, "Retention and Intention in Massive Open Online Courses: In Depth," *Educause Review Online*, June 3, 2013, available at http://www.educause.edu/ero/article/ retention-and-intention-massive-open-online-courses-depth-0.

2. Research results from HarvardX are available at http://harvardx.harvard .edu/research. Corresponding research and results for MITx courses are available at http://odl.mit.edu/mitx-working-papers/.

3. Interview with author.

4. See J. DeBoer, Andrew D. Ho, Glenda S. Stump, and Lor Breslow, "Changing 'Course': Reconceptualizing Educational Variables for Massive Open Online Courses," Massachusetts Institute of Technology and Harvard Graduate School of Education, available at http://tll.mit.edu/sites/default/files/library/ Changing_Course.pdf.

5. See Kalyan Veeramachaneni, Franck Dernoncourt, Colin Taylor, Zachary Pardos, and Una-May O'Reilly, "MOOCdb: Developing Data Standards for MOOC Data Science," Massachusetts Institute of Technology (working paper–2013), available at http://groups.csail.mit.edu/EVO-DesignOpt/groupWebSite /uploads/Site/MoocshopCamera.pdf.

6. Information on the new journal, published by Mary Ann Liebert, Inc. Publishers and edited by Nishikant Sonwalkar is available at http://www.liebert pub.com/overview/moocs-forum/619/.

7. Information on the MOOC research initiative is available at http://www .moocresearch.com/ and a list of the first recipients of grants for the research program is available at http://www.moocresearch.com/mooc-research-initiative-grants-awarded.

8. See Glenda Stump, Jennifer DeBoer, Jonathan Whittinghill, and Lori Breslow, "Development of a Framework to Classify MOOC Discussion Forum Posts: Methodology and Challenges," Massachusetts Institute of Technology and Harvard Graduate School of Education (working paper–2013), available at http://tll.mit.edu/sites/default/files/library/Coding_a_MOOC_Discussion _Forum.pdf.

9. See R. J. Clougherty Jr. and Viktoria Popova, "Crowdsourcing to Assess MOOCs: A Position Paper," *MOOCs Forum* 1, no. 1 (2013): 10–13.

10. A summary of results from the study is available at http://www.sjsu.edu/ chemistry/People/Faculty/Collins_Research_Page/index.html and a detailed report of preliminary findings is available at http://www.sjsu.edu/chemistry/ People/Faculty/Collins_Research_Page/AOLE%20Report%20-September%20 10%202013%20final.pdf.

11. See Pat Lopes Harris, "SJSU/EdX Adds More Campuses, Courses," *SJSU Today* (blog), April 10, 2013, available at http://blogs.sjsu.edu/today/2013/ sjsuedx-expansion/.

12. See Carl Straumsheim, "Scaling Back in San Jose," *Inside Higher Ed*, September 18, 2013, available at http://www.insidehighered.com/news/2013/12/18/san -jose-state-u-resurrects-scaled-back-online-course-experiment-mooc-provider.

13. Interview with author.

14. I am using a definition of "crowdsourcing" developed in Daren Brabham's 2013 book on the subject (Daren C. Brabham, *Crowdsourcing* [Cambridge, MA: MIT Press, 2013]).

15. Cathy N. Davidson, *How Technology and Brain Science Will Transform Schools and Business for the 21st Century* (New York: Viking, 2011). Additional information on Dr. Davidson's work is available at http://cathydavidson .com/.

16. Cathy N. Davidson, interview with author, Degree of Freedom Podcast (August 2, 2013), available at http://degreeoffreedom.org/interview-with-cathy-davidson/.

17. David Cox, interview with author, Degree of Freedom Podcast (September 20, 2013), available at http://degreeoffreedom.org/interview-david-cox-creator-harvardxs-fundamentals-neuroscience-mooc/.

18. See "What Went Wrong with AllLearn?" *University Business*, June 2006, available at http://www.universitybusiness.com/article/what-went-wrong-alllearn.

19. An overview of Online X, part of MIT's professional education service, is available at http://web.mit.edu/professional/onlinex-programs/overview.html.

20. See Gregory Ferenstein, "Coursera Launches an Online Vocational Mini-Credential Taught by Top Colleges," *TechCrunch*, January 21, 2014, available at http://techcrunch.com/2014/01/21/coursera-launches-an-online-vocational-mini-credential-taught-by-top-colleges/.

21. For example, Coursera's description of early Signature Track customers for a UC–San Francisco nutrition course included a chef, two coaches, and a physical therapist who planned to use the new credential to support business and career goals. A blog entry describing these Signature Track students is available at http://blog.coursera.org/post/48598266910/congrats-to-the-first-students-to-earn-verified.

22. See Steve Kolowich, "MOOCs for Credit," *Inside Higher Ed*, October 29, 2012, available at http://www.insidehighered.com/news/2012/10/29/coursera-strikes-mooc-licensing-deal-antioch-university.

23. See Steve Kolowich, "How edX Plans to Earn, and Share, Revenue from Its Free Online Courses," *Chronicle of Higher Education*, February 21, 2013, available at http://chronicle.com/article/How-EdX-Plans-to-Earn-and/137433/.

24. For example, Kevin deLaplante, professor of philosophy at Iowa State University, used a set of lecture videos he created for students as the content for his Critical Thinker Academy (www.criticalthinkeracademy.com), which offers free access to some lectures as well as access to more content through a paid course via the online vendor Udemy.

25. See "Elsevier to Provide Textbooks for Five New edX MOOCs" (press release), October 23, 2013, available at http://www.elsevier.com/about/press-releases/science-and-technology/elsevier-to-provide-textbooks-for-five-new-edx-moocs.

26. See Salman Khan, "Let's Use Video to Reinvent Education," Ted Talks, March 2011, available at http://www.ted.com/talks/salman_khan_let_s_use_video_to_reinvent_education.html.

27. During a stint as executive editor at one of the major educational publishers specializing in the teaching of computer skills, I oversaw a product used to provide automated assessment and training to students that, in conjunction with a textbook, moved the bulk of instruction out of the classroom with class time dedicated to individual projects and group work.

Chapter 6

1. See Max Chafkin, "Udacity's Sebastian Thrun, Godfather of Free Online Education, Changes Course." *Fast Company*, November 14, 2013, available at http://www.fastcompany.com/3021473/udacity-sebastian-thrun-uphill-climb.

2. See Rebecca Schuman, "The King of MOOCs Abdicates the Throne," *Slate*, November 19, 2013, available at http://www.slate.com/articles/life/education/2013/11/sebastian_thrun_and_udacity_distance_learning_is_unsuccessful_for_most_students.html.

3. A list of colleges that have partnered with Straighterline to accept their online courses for credit is available at http://www.straighterline.com/colleges/partner-colleges/partner-colleges-home/.

4. An information graphic containing gap year statistics for the United Kingdom is available at http://visual.ly/gap-year-statistics-broaden-your-mind. See also Alina Tugend, "Bridging the Gap between High School and College, at a Price," *New York Times*, p. B4, October 5, 2013, available at http://www.nytimes.com/2013/10/05/your-money/an-often-costly-year-to-bridge-the-gap-between-high-school-and-college.html.

5. See "Reinventing Public Higher Education—A Call to Action," San Jose State University—Office of the President, available at http://www.sjsu.edu/president/docs/reinventinghighered_full.pdf.

6. As an illustration of how much enthusiasm for a class cannot be captured in initial enrollment and completion statistics, Professor Nagy's invitation to students who had completed the first iteration of Ancient Greek Hero to take the course again when it was repeated a few months later drew over 4,000 repeat participants, including over 400 who had previously earned a certificate. Gross statistics also fail to capture the engagement of individual students, a zeal that led at least one student (me, as it happens) to inquire if he was the first person to have ever read Homer's *Odyssey* in the men's room of a Valvoline.

7. See Phillip J. O'Connell, "Adults in Training: An International Comparison of Continuing Education and Training," Organization for Economic Co-operation and Development, 1999, available at http://search.oecd.org/officialdocuments/publicdisplaydocumentpdf/?cote=CERI/WD(99)1&docLanguage=En.

8. A list of Osher Lifelong Learning Institutes is available at http://www.osherfoundation.org/index.php?olli_list.

9. See Peter Murray, "Sebastian Thrun Aims to Revolutionize University Education with Udacity." *SingularityHUB* (blog), January 28, 2012, available at http://singularityhub.com/2012/01/28/sebastian-thrun-aims-to-revolutionize-university-education-with-udacity/.

10. See Laura Pappano, "The Boy Genius of Ulan Bator," *New York Times Magazine*, September 13, 2013, available at http://www.nytimes.com/2013/09/15/magazine/the-boy-genius-of-ulan-bator.html.

11. A list of speakers who participated in the 2013 LINC conference (along with copies of their presentations) is available at http://linc.mit.edu/linc2013/speakers.html.

12. An author interview with Katie Cleary, one of the leaders of MOOC Campus (which includes background information on the original Black Mountain College experiment), is available at http://degreeoffreedom.org/interview-with-katie-cleary-community-director-at-mooc-campus/.

13. Clayton Christensen, Michael B. Horn, and Curtis W. Johnson, *Disrupting Class: How Disruptive Innovation Will Change the Way the World Learns* (New York: McGraw Hill, 2008).

A LIST OF MOOC PROVIDERS MENTIONED IN THIS BOOK

Canvas
www.canvas.net

Coursera
www.coursera.org

edX
www.edx.org

FutureLearn
www.futurelearn.com

iversity
www.iversity.org

MOOC.org
www.mooc.org

Novoed
www.novoed.com

Udacity
www.udacity.com

Udemy
www.udemy.com

ADDITIONAL RESOURCES

Jeffrey R. Young, *Beyond the MOOC Hype: A Guide to Education's High-Tech Disruption* (Chronicle of Higher Education (2013).

What You Need to Know About MOOCs—A timeline of Chronicle stories on the MOOC phenomenon, available at http://chronicle.com/article/What-You-Need-to-Know-About/133475/.

MOOC News and Reviews—News coverage and course reviews for massive online classes, available at www.moocnewsandreviews.com.

Degree of Freedom blog—The author's regular writing on the subject of MOOCs and free learning, available at www.degreeoffreedom.org

Degree of Freedom Podcast—Interviews with MOOC leaders, professors and students on topics related to massive online classes, available at https://itunes.apple.com/us/podcast/degree-freedom-podcast-feed/id657605401.

Degree of Freedom Portfolio—A portfolio of work products related to the author's Degree of Freedom One Year BA project, available at https://www.accredible.com/u/JonathanHaber. (**Note**: this portfolio was put together using the Accredible platform, available at www.accredible.com.)